Magna Carta

THE HERITAGE OF LIBERTY

BY

ANNE PALLISTER

OXFORD

AT THE CLARENDON PRESS

1971

Oxford University Press, Ely House, London W. 1

GLASGOW NEW YORK TORONTO MELBOURNE WELLINGTON
CAPE TOWN SALISBURY IBADAN NAIROBI DAR ES SALAAM LUSAKA ADDIS ABABA
BOMBAY CALCUTTA MADRAS KARACHI LAHORE DACCA
KUALA LUMPUR SINGAPORE HONG KONG TOKYO

PRINTED IN GREAT BRITAIN

*For my mother
and in memory of
my father*

Preface

MAGNA CARTA is often regarded as the nearest equivalent to a written constitution which the English possess. It is held in esteem as a statement of individual liberties which are beyond the interference of the state. It is synonymous with responsible government and equitable justice. So deeply rooted is this belief in the Charter that neither modern critical examination of the original document nor the removal of all but four of its clauses from the statute-book has seriously weakened its hold over the popular imagination. Indeed, Magna Carta is a firmly established part of our national heritage. This book is an attempt to analyse the importance of the Charter in English political thought and practice since the seventeenth century, to explain its remarkable persistence, and to assess its value today.

I was first encouraged to investigate the 'myth' of Magna Carta by Professor J. C. Holt, whose scholarly work has added new dimensions to our knowledge of the Charter of 1215. I am deeply grateful to him for his continued encouragement, interest, and advice. He very kindly read the work in typescript and made many valuable comments and criticisms. On legal questions I have benefited from discussions with Mr. D. G. T. Williams, who read the typescript of Chapter 7 and was generous with advice on modern law. I am indebted to Professor W. R. Fryer, Sir Herbert Butterfield, Mr. E. A. Smith, and Dr. B. R. Kemp for their help and interest, and to Mr. W. J. Messer for assistance with proof-reading. The work was completed during a sabbatical term spent in Cambridge and I am grateful to the University of Reading and University College, Cambridge, for making this possible.

A. P.

Reading
February 1971

Contents

List of Plates

Abbreviations

A.C.	Appeal Court
Add. MSS.	British Museum, Additional Manuscripts
All E.R.	All England Reports
Am. H.R.	*American Historical Review*
App.	Appendix
B.M.	British Museum
Ch.	Chancery
C.J.	*Commons' Journals*
Cmnd.	Command
C.S.P.D.	*Calendar of State Papers, Domestic*
D.N.B.	*Dictionary of National Biography*
E.H.R.	*English Historical Review*
Harl. Misc.	*Harleian Miscellany* (1808–13)
H.M.C.	Historical Manuscripts Commission
K.B.	King's Bench
Law Com.	Law Commission Papers
L.J.	*Lords' Journals*
L.Q.R.	*Law Quarterly Review*
L.R.	Law Reports
N.B.	*The North Briton*, compiled W. Bingley (2nd edn., 1771)
P.D.	Hansard, *Parliamentary Debates*
P.H.	Cobbett, *Parliamentary History from 1066 to 1803* (1806–20)
P.P.	Parliamentary Papers
Somers	*Somers Tracts* (2nd edn., 1809–15)
S.T.	*State Trials*, ed. T. B. and T. J. Howell (1816–28)
State Tracts	*State Tracts, being a collection of several treatises relating to Government, 1660–1689* (1689–92)
T.L.R.	Times Law Reports
W.L.R.	Weekly Law Reports

I

Introduction

VENERATION of Magna Carta is a long-established national tradition in England. For more than seven centuries Englishmen have eulogized the Charter as both the foundation of their liberties and their best safeguard against arbitrary governmental interference with individual freedom. More generally, the principles which men have believed to be embodied in the Charter can be found reiterated and revered throughout the English-speaking world. Lord Denning expressed a widely held view when he described Magna Carta, during the celebrations commemorating its seven hundred and fiftieth anniversary, as 'the greatest constitutional document of all times— the foundation of the freedom of the individual against the arbitrary authority of the despot'.[1]

But how and why has this belief developed, and how much substance now remains beneath such a statement? The historian who attempts to investigate this phenomenon, the 'myth' of Magna Carta, is faced with a number of problems. Because of the pervasive nature of the myth, a wide variety of seemingly unrelated material must be studied over a long period of time, thereby giving rise to dangers of generalization, distortion, and superficiality. Throughout this multiformity of material, belief in and respect for the Charter is clearly evident, but it is more often assumed or formally expressed than explained or justified. To complicate the task still further, there is no definitive interpretation of the Charter, indeed there never has been. The 1215 Charter of King John was itself a

---

[1] *Guardian*, 1 June 1956.

B

reinterpretation and assertion of ancient custom;[1] it was, as Samuel Johnson picturesquely put it, 'born with a grey Beard'.[2] The subsequent history of the Charter has been one of continual interpretation and development, for each generation has written its own history of the Charter according to the needs of the day. The English, perhaps more than continental nations, have always looked to the past and been influenced by their interpretation of that past. From earliest times English reformers have tried to show that they were not innovators but rather restorers of ancient and true ways which had been lost. The barons who opposed King John called for the restoration of the liberties enjoyed under Edward the Confessor and Henry I. They looked back to an idealized past in which men enjoyed all their rights and liberties and where government was according to law, and they demanded a return to this good and ancient practice. By enumerating ancient rights in the Charter, the barons were attempting to place permanent limitations upon the power of the crown in future, and by 1237, when Henry III confirmed the liberties contained in the Charter in perpetuity, they had been successful; they had converted their interpretation of custom into undisputed law.[3] From this time, Magna Carta was regarded as fundamental and inalienable law, limiting upon and superior to the crown, and its repeated confirmations in the thirteenth and fourteenth centuries further enhanced its position as higher law.[4]

In the fifteenth and sixteenth centuries the Charter declined in importance, but it was revived in a striking fashion in the early seventeenth century.[5] The man most responsible for the

---

[1] J. C. Holt, *Magna Carta* (Cambridge, 1965) and 'Magna Carta: Law and Constitution', *Listener*, 8 July 1965.

[2] *The Second Part of the Confutation of the Ballancing Letter* (1700), 2.

[3] Holt, *Magna Carta*, and 'Magna Carta and the Origin of Statute Law', *Essays in Honour of Gaines Post*, ed. D. E. Queller (Princeton, N.J., forthcoming).

[4] F. Thompson, *The First Century of Magna Carta: Why it Persisted as a Document* (Minneapolis, 1925), and *Magna Carta: Its Role in the Making of the English Constitution, 1300–1629* (Minneapolis, 1948).

[5] Thompson, *Magna Carta*, and H. Butterfield, *Magna Carta in the Historiography of the Sixteenth and Seventeenth Centuries* (Reading, Stenton Lecture, 1969).

new interest in the Charter was Sir Edward Coke, who drew heavily upon the past in his criticism of the policies and methods of the Stuart government. Coke eulogized the Charter as 'declaratory of the principal grounds of the fundamental laws of England',[1] and he and his fellow parliamentarians demanded from Charles I a restoration of the ancient liberties expressed in the Charter. Their demand was to be reiterated by the Levellers, the whigs at the Glorious Revolution, the parliamentary reformers of the eighteenth century, and the Chartists of the nineteenth century. Thus, throughout its history, Magna Carta has been 'a rallying cry and a protecting bulwark in every crisis which threatened to endanger the national liberties'.[2] In origin a limited document relating to certain specific feudal rights, the Charter gradually came to be revered as the source of a vast conglomeration of ancient rights and liberties which were regarded as the 'birthright' of the English people. If, as Sir Herbert Butterfield has suggested, the theme of English political history is the story of our liberty,[3] then the whole of English political history is also the story of the unfolding of the 'myth' of Magna Carta.

But the concept of the Charter as the embodiment of ancient and inviolable liberties has not gone uncriticized. The first blow came in the mid seventeenth century, shortly after its revival by Coke. The events of these years undermined the old belief in higher law as a limitation upon the action of governments; men now began to emphasize the sanctions rather than the sources of law and to point out that laws made and enforced by governments cannot bind governments.[4] At the same time, customary law was rejected as partial and inadequate in comparison with the wider, indeed unlimited, claims based upon abstract natural rights, and individual rights were claimed on grounds not of past precedent but of reason and equity.[5]

[1] 2 *Institutes* (1797), Proeme.
[2] W. S. McKechnie, *Magna Carta* (Glasgow, 2nd edn., 1924), 154.
[3] *The Englishman and his History* (Cambridge, 1944), 3.
[4] For example, Robert Filmer and Thomas Hobbes, see below, pp. 24–5.
[5] By William Walwyn and Richard Overton, see below, pp. 18 ff.

The equation of the Charter with immemorial customary law was also attacked on historical grounds. In the late seventeenth century Robert Brady showed it to be historically unfounded and regretted that 'in spite of *Truth* and *Matter of Fact*, we find nothing in our Common *Histories* of these Times, but the *Brave Feats* performed by the *English* for their Fundamental Rights and Liberties'.[1] As historical techniques improved in the eighteenth century, it became increasingly difficult to reconcile the belief that Magna Carta enunciated immemorial liberties with known historical fact. Finally, the rise of practical parliamentary sovereignty prepared the way for theories which were inconsistent with the old emphasis on the Charter. Parliament, which had risen to power as the guardian of the law against the arbitrary pretensions of the monarchy, began to exercise the right to interpret and refashion all law. The theoretical justification of parliamentary sovereignty provided by the Utilitarians undermined the philosophical foundations of the 'myth' and opened the way for the mutilation and reduction of the Charter at the hands of its former defenders, the lawyers in parliament.

Yet Magna Carta has survived all these attacks. Divorced from both its historical setting and its statutory enactment, the Charter continues to enunciate political and legal principles which are as important today as in the thirteenth or seventeenth centuries. The equation of law and liberty, the belief that the law of England protects rather than restricts the freedom of the individual, which is the central feature of the Charter, still lies at the heart of English political and legal thought and practice; and the Charter provides a standard of political ethos against which official action in its effects upon the individual can be measured.

In addition, belief in an ancient customary law protecting the individual in the possession of his rights and liberties and limiting the competence of the state has been a remarkably

---

[1] *A Complete History of England* (1685), Preface to the Reader, unpaginated.

constant feature throughout English political thought. Few theorists have been able to free themselves completely from this tradition, although many have tried. Henry Parker, while condemning the prevailing dependence upon the common law in the mid seventeenth century, still regarded governments as limited by fundamental law. Richard Overton, who dismissed the past and turned to abstract natural law, continued on occasion to make use of the old arguments based upon customary law and the Charter. In the eighteenth century the parliamentary reformers clung to historical arguments despite the difficulties this involved; indeed, many saw themselves as successors to the barons who secured Magna Carta. Even those more radical reformers who were influenced by the ideas of the French Revolution still opposed arbitrary governmental action on grounds of clause 29 of the Charter. Advocates of parliamentary sovereignty also found it difficult to discard the old theory of customary law. William Blackstone reiterated the Cokean interpretation of the Charter as the enunciation of ancient law, and always assumed that parliament would respect this law. Jeremy Bentham, despite his scorn for the achievements of the past, never abandoned the legal principles expressed in Magna Carta. Indeed, when it came to attacking specific abuses in the legal system of his own day, Bentham turned to the Charter rather than the principle of utility. Bentham exemplifies the curious ambivalence which pervades modern English political thought. Determined to formulate a new and original theory, Bentham was never able to free himself from the ideas, the inheritance, of the past. Few have succeeded where Bentham failed, and even fewer have managed to discard Magna Carta, which has been a major stumbling-block in the formulation of abstract political theory.

De Lolme commented in the eighteenth century on the English reverence for the past; he noted:

there was a far greater probability of success, in raising among the [English] people the notions (familiar to them) of legal claims and long-established customs, than in arguing with them from the no less rational, but less determinate and somewhat dangerous doctrines, concerning the original rights of Mankind.[1]

Magna Carta is the compendium of 'long-established customs'; it enunciates principles of responsible government and equitable justice which have been claimed, if not practised, longer than the Charter itself has been in existence, and it states these principles as the ancient and undoubted heritage of the English people. Regardless of whether this is historically verifiable, the fact remains that for more than seven centuries the Charter has been so interpreted, and its survival is a living illustration of that characteristic of the English nation which Edmund Burke called a 'powerful prepossession towards antiquity'.[2]

Historical fact has been compared to a grain of sand within the shell of a pearl oyster; 'about it are deposited the ensphering layers of myth and legend till a glimmering treasure is produced that excites the mightiest passions of men'.[3] The remainder of this work is an attempt to trace and explain the growth, development, and transfiguration of 'one special Pearl'[4]—Magna Carta.

[1] *The Constitution of England* (1775), 9 n.
[2] *Reflexions on the Revolution in France* (1790), *Works* (1808), v. 76.
[3] W. A. Dunning, 'Truth in History', 19 *Am. H.R.* (1924), 220.
[4] J. Lilburne, *An Hue and Cry after the Fundamental Lawes and Liberties of England* (1653), 4.

2

Prerogative, Liberty, and the Charter

The Law is the Boundary, the Measure betwixt the King's
Prerogative, and the Peoples Liberty; whilst these move in
their own Orbs, they are a support and a security to one
another; the Prerogative a Cover and Defence to the Liberty
of the People; and the People, by their Liberty, are enabled
to be a Foundation to the Prerogative: but if these Bounds
be so removed, that they enter into Contestation and Conflict,
one of these Mischiefs must ensue: If the Prerogative of the
King overwhelm the Liberty of the People, it will be turned
into Tyranny; if Liberty undermine the Prerogative, it will
grow into Anarchy.[1]

JOHN PYM's warning about the consequences of tampering
with the traditional, legally balanced constitution was verified
during the middle decades of the seventeenth century. Pym
himself was one of the leading defenders of the 'liberty of the
people' against what he and his fellow parliamentarians regarded as the dangerous and arbitrary extension of the prerogative by the Stuart monarchy. Yet in his zeal to limit
the prerogative, Pym began to make unprecedented and far-
reaching claims for parliament, claims which seemed to Charles I
and the royalists to 'undermine the prerogative'. The result was
civil war, and in the period of confusion prior to and during
the war the English gave renewed thought to political problems.

The seventeenth century was an age dominated as much by
law and history as by religion and, as many royalist and parliamentarian propagandists were men with legal training, it is
hardly surprising that Magna Carta was cited and debated

---

[1] John Pym, Trial of Strafford (1641), Rushworth, *Historical Collections* (1721),
viii. 662.

alongside the Bible. The trial of Archbishop Laud illustrates the way in which both sides appealed to the Charter in support of their cause. In January 1645 Laud was accused of having attempted to overthrow the laws of England, and a paper on the subject of subsidies was produced in evidence; this contained the comment, in Laud's handwriting, 'the Great Charter had an obscure birth from usurpation, and was fostered and shewed to the world by rebellion'.[1] After denying his authorship of the remark in question, which in fact is taken from Sir Walter Raleigh's *The Prerogative of Parliament*, Laud sensibly observed: 'Nor is this now any disgrace to Magna Carta, that it had an obscure birth; for say the difficulties of the times brought it obscurely forth; there's no blemish to the credit and honour to which it hath for many ages attained.'[2] Indeed it was to this very Charter which Laud was accused of scorning that an anonymous apologist appealed in the Archbishop's defence. He complained:

It is a fundamental law of the English Government, and the first article in the Magna Carta, that the church of England shall be free, and shall have her whole rights and privileges inviolable;

yet bishops were illegally voted out of parliament in order to secure the parliamentary condemnation of Laud.

It is a fundamental law of the English liberty that no free man shall be taken or imprisoned without cause shewne, or be detained without being brought unto his answer, in due form of law;

yet Laud was imprisoned without charge.

It is a fundamental law of the English Government that no man be disseised of his freehold or liberties, but by the known lawes of the land;

yet Laud was deprived of his land, jurisdiction, and rights.

It is a fundamental law of the English liberty that no man shall be

---

[1] Laud, *Works*, ed. W. Scott and J. Bliss (Oxford, 1847–60), vii. 127–8.
[2] Ibid. iv. 364.

condemned, or put to death, but by the lawful judgment of his peeres, or by the law of the land;

yet Laud was denied this.[1]

Here, the author has turned the parliamentarian arguments of individual rights and equality of justice against the actions of parliament itself. He condemns their procedure against Laud as illegal according to their own principles, and his argument is based on Magna Carta, especially clause 29, which could be used, and indeed was extensively used, to oppose any infringement of justice by whatever person or party. Yet the very nature and origin of the Great Charter, as Raleigh commented and Laud significantly transcribed, made it a dangerous precedent for the royalist party. A Charter of liberties forced upon a reluctant king by his rebellious subjects was, in the light of the political situation in the 1640s, a precedent which many royalists preferred to ignore. The difficulty of accepting the liberties contained in the Charter without seeming to approve or condone the means by which they were achieved, remained a serious obstacle in royalist political thought up to the 1680s, when an attempt was made to solve the dilemma.[2]

During the Civil War, appeal to the Charter reached its height within the parliamentary opposition. The lawyers and gentry of the Commons, during their long conflict with James I and Charles I, gradually built up a case based upon the concept of the subordination of the crown to the law, with a revived insistence on the role of parliament as the guardian of that law, an argument which they derived from Sir Edward Coke. During the last twenty-eight years of his long and eventful career, Coke was the champion of the common law and the common law courts. At a time when the Stuart monarchy was making increasing use of its prerogative powers, Coke insisted on the supremacy of the common law: 'It is a Maxim, The Common-Law hath admeasured the King's prerogative' he

---

[1] *A Briefe Relation of the Death and Sufferings of the Most Reverend and Renowned Prelate, the Lord Archbishop of Canterbury, Somers*, iv. 447.

[2] See below, pp. 33 ff.

told the House of Commons in 1628.[1] This belief that the common law exists to protect the individual is the key to Coke's view of law. Deriving his argument from an unreliable legal text of the late thirteenth century,[2] Coke eulogized Magna Carta as the embodiment of the ancient and pure laws of Anglo-Saxon England, regained after their destruction by the Normans. He spoke of the 'great weightinesse and weightie greatnesse' of the contents of the Charter, which he believed to be 'the fountaine of all the fundamentall lawes of the realm . . . [and] a confirmation or restitution of the common law'.[3] To Coke, common law was an essential safeguard for the liberties of the people against the arbitrary extension of the prerogative.

Such opinions not unnaturally antagonized the Stuarts. In 1616 Coke was dismissed from his office of Chief Justice of the King's Bench;[4] in 1622 he was imprisoned in the Tower for almost seven months after playing a leading part in the opposition to James in the parliament of 1621; he was active in the parliament of 1624 and closely involved in drawing up the Petition of Right in the parliament of 1628. After the dissolution of this last parliament, Coke withdrew from politics, but three years later he again aroused the fears of the Stuart government for it was reported that he was working on a book 'concerning Magna Carta'.[5] Aware of Coke's enormous influence, Charles I quickly ordered the suppression of this work.[6] In September 1634, when Coke was dying, his house and his chambers were ransacked on orders from the Privy Council and a number of manuscripts 'of great consideration and weight' were seized.[7] Thus it is clear that both James and

---

[1] Rushworth, op. cit. i. 512.
[2] *Mirror of Justices*, probably written by Andrew Horn *c.* 1285–90.
[3] 1 *Institutes*, 81a. This work is a commentary on Littleton's *Tenures*.
[4] He had been appointed in 1613, after being Chief Justice of the Common Pleas since 1606.
[5] Sir Thomas Barrington to his wife (H.M.C., *7th Report*, App. i. 548). This was to be published in 1642 as 2 *Institutes*, see below, p. 11.
[6] *C.S.P.D.* 1629–31, 490.
[7] These included the manuscripts of 2, 3, and 4 *Institutes*; *C.S.P.D.* 1634–5,

Charles realized the dangers to their position inherent in Coke's views, and they took positive steps to silence him. Their efforts were short-lived, however, for in 1640 the Long Parliament ordered the recovery and publication of Coke's confiscated papers, and as a consequence his commentary on Magna Carta was published in 1642.[1] This work had a far-reaching influence upon parliamentarian thought, and numerous references to Coke and the Great Charter can be found in the debates and the statutes of the Long Parliament.[2]

Initially, the members of the Long Parliament were united in upholding Coke's doctrine that the liberties of England were immemorial and protected by fundamental law. They believed the main task of parliament to be the defence of this ancient law expressed in Magna Carta against the arbitrary ambition of the Stuarts. Yet faced with fighting a war against the king, the parliamentary party was compelled to free itself from the limitations that law placed upon its activity. Parliament now began to assert the right to interpret the fundamental laws of the kingdom which previously it had merely claimed to defend. In 1644 Charles Herle declared that parliament, as 'the highest Court, from which there lies no appeale, must needs have the *finall judgment* of what is *Law*, or els there must be no such *judgment*'.[3] This right of interpretation was easily extendible to include the right to make and set aside law at parliament's pleasure, and the constitutional doctrine that parliament was the final interpreter of the fundamental laws of the land enabled the Long Parliament to move away from Coke's belief in the supremacy of law towards a new doctrine of the sovereignty of parliament. It was the development of this latter doctrine which divided the opponents of Charles I. Thus interpretation

163. See also R. Coke, *A Detection of the Court and State of England during the four last reigns and Interregnum* (1694), i. 354.

[1] *C.J.* ii. 45–6. See above, p. 10. Two years later 3 and 4 *Institutes* were published.

[2] For example, the Act for the Abolition of the Court of Star Chamber. See also *Journal of Sir Simonds D'Ewes*, ed. W. Notestein (New Haven, Conn., 1923).

[3] *Ahab's Fall by his Prophets Flatteries* (1644), 36.

of Magna Carta is an index of the growing divergence of political ideas within the parliamentary opposition.

The writings of Henry Parker most clearly illustrate the new parliamentary claim.[1] Parker consciously rejected the prevailing dependence upon the common law, declaring 'Nothing has done us more harme of late, than this opinion of adhering to Law only for our preservation.'[2] Laws, he argued, are not enough in themselves, but need to be explained and enforced for 'what a livelesse fond thing would Law be, without any judge to determine it, or power to enforce it'.[3] Parker stressed the necessity for a clearly known authority in every state in order to maintain unity and enforce law. He insisted: 'Supreme power ought to be intire and undivided, and cannot else be sufficient for the protection of all, if it doe not extend over all; without any other equall power to controll, or diminish it.'[4] He attributed this supreme and arbitrary power to parliament because he felt that such power could be dangerous in the hands of one man but not in the hands of parliament, which 'is neither one nor few, it is indeed the State itself'.[5] This is the basis of Parker's thought; parliament and the state are inseparable, if not synonymous. There can be no theoretical limits or restraints upon the power of parliament for 'all the right of the King and people, depends upon their pleasure'.[6] Indeed, Parker argued that parliament, if it were not responsible, which of course it is, might grant the king the despotic power which he sought, and even 'abridge the freedom of the Subject . . . [and] repeale our great Charter'.[7]

In the light of such statements, it is hardly surprising that Parker has been called the first writer in English history to

---

[1] Professor W. K. Jordan describes Parker as 'the most original, and possibly the most important political theorist of the revolutionary era' (*Men of Substance* (Chicago, 1942), 140). Parker exercised a considerable influence upon Thomas Hobbes.

[2] *Contra Replicant* (1643), 19.

[3] *Observations upon some of his Majesties late Answers and Expresses* (1642), 13–14.

[4] *The True Grounds of Ecclesiastical Regiment* (1641), 8.

[5] *Observations*, 34.   [6] Ibid. 45.

[7] *Contra Replicant*, 30.

advance a theory of parliamentary sovereignty.[1] Yet this aspect of his thought should not be over-stressed. He certainly advocated parliamentary sovereignty in the chaotic circumstances of his time, but he did not think of parliament as exercising such power in more orderly, normal conditions. He stated this quite clearly when he wrote 'this power [of parliament] is not claimed as ordinary; nor to any purpose, But to save the Kingdom from ruine'.[2] He still retained a belief in fundamental law although he identified it, not with custom or statute, but as part of the overriding law of nature inherent in every individual:

Fundamental law is such a one as is coucht radically in Nature itself (and so becomes the very pin of law and society) and is written and enacted irrepealably in her *Magna charta*, which we are not beholden to any sublunary power for, but belongs to us as we are living and sociable creatures. And no Knowne act . . . can clash with this, but must in equitie vail to it, as to its superintendent.[3]

Parliament is bound to uphold this fundamental law and to defend the natural rights of the people against arbitrary encroachment from the crown. Parker was thus a realist who saw the need for extraordinary power in extraordinary times rather than the founder of the modern doctrine of parliamentary sovereignty. Even so, few of his contemporaries were prepared to press the claims of parliament as far as Parker. Indeed, when the Presbyterian-dominated Long Parliament attempted to force its views of government upon the nation in the late 1640s, it aroused violent and outspoken opposition on the traditional grounds of individual rights and the supremacy of law.

In particular, the Independents and Levellers within the army allied together to oppose this new parliamentary tyranny. However, this proved a tenuous alliance, for the Independents were essentially conservative in outlook, with a deep respect

---

[1] M. A. Judson, 'Henry Parker and the Theory of Parliamentary Sovereignty' in *Essays in History and Political Theory in Honour of C. H. McIlwain* (Cambridge, Mass., 1936), 138–67.

[2] *Observations*, 45.

[3] *Animadversions Animadverted* (1642), 3.

for property, whilst the Levellers were more radical, concerned not only to safeguard but also to extend civil and political liberties. Their aim was 'the right, freedome, safety, and well-being of every particular man, woman, and child in England'.[1] The Putney debates of October and November 1647 demonstrated that while both groups believed in the supremacy of law, they differed in their interpretation of that law. The Levellers saw it as a means of limiting the government in the interests of the people, 'to keep rulers within the bounds of just and righteous government'.[2] To the Independents, law was necessary for the maintenance of the existing social order based upon property. Ireton defined law as 'made by those people that have a property, a fixt property, in the land', and he firmly believed government by the propertied classes to be 'more prudent and safe'.[3] It is hardly surprising, therefore, that the alliance between these fundamentally opposed groups was short-lived. The Putney debates ended in deadlock, and the Levellers subsequently became more desperate and revolutionary in their language, the Independents more conservative and fearful of social revolution.

The Independents, while paying the traditional lip-service to the Charter, in fact made little novel or significant use of it. One explanation for the absence of the Charter from their political thought may be that it had become, by this time, a radical document closely identified with the dangerous Leveller party and the popular press and therefore to be ignored by more conservative politicians.

The Levellers certainly used the Great Charter abundantly, and in a far more positive manner than their contemporaries. Many Englishmen drew upon the Charter to defend existing

[1] J. Lilburne, *The Just Defence* (1653), W. Haller and G. Davies, *The Leveller Tracts, 1647–53* (New York, 1944), 453. Professor C. B. Macpherson points out, however, that the Levellers excluded two substantial categories of men from their franchise proposals, (i) wage-earners or servants and (ii) those in receipt of alms: *The Political Theory of Possessive Individualism* (Oxford, 1962), 106–59.

[2] J. Ware, *The Corruption and Deficiency of the Laws of England* (1649), *Harl. Misc.* iii. 251.

[3] *Clarke Papers*, ed. C. H. Firth (1891), i. 319 and 334.

privileges from encroachment, but only the Levellers developed a constructive programme of reform based upon Magna Carta, which they elevated to the status of a political bible, extending and deepening its recent significance by raising it from a mere antimonarchical document to be the safeguard of the rights and privileges of all Englishmen against encroachment from any other quarter also. As an anonymous writer proclaimed: 'This *Charter* of our Liberties, or Freemans *Birthright* . . . is that brazen wall, and impregnable Bulwark that defends the Common liberty of *England* from an illegal and destructive *Arbitrary Power* whatsoever, be it either by *Prince* or *State* endeavoured.'[1] The Levellers used the Charter to justify their resistance to arbitrary government of any kind. They rebelled against Charles I because he 'walked contrary to Magna Carta and the Petition of Right, and oppressed them contrary to the true intent and meaning thereof'. They supported the attack upon Strafford and Laud because 'they trod Magna Carta . . . under their feet, and indeavoured to rule by their own wills, and so set up an arbitrary government'.[2]

At first the Levellers placed their hopes in the House of Commons, urging its members to reform the political, social, and legal systems, to uphold Magna Carta and restore the people to their ancient and rightful liberties. But as their demands and petitions went unanswered and their disillusionment grew, they began to extend their doctrine of resistance against the Long Parliament. They now began to argue that just as kings are responsible to the law and Magna Carta, so too are parliaments, and declared that 'the Parliament is not without a law and rule, nor may doe what they will, nor anything . . . contrary to the fundamentall Lawes and constitutions of the Kingdome'.[3] They condemned the Long Parliament as 'a company of traytors and tyrants' and urged resistance in

---

[1] *Vox Plebis* (1646), 9. This tract has been variously attributed to Henry Marten, Richard Overton, and John Lilburne, but it is probably the work of Marten.

[2] J. Lilburne, *A Copy of a Letter to a Friend* (1645), 16.

[3] Anon., *Plain Truth, without Feare or Flattery* (1647), 15.

defence of the Charter.[1] Anticipating Locke, they asserted that it was the duty of parliament to protect the rights and liberties of the people of England, from whom their power derived: 'Sure and stable is this principle, "Salus Populi est Suprema Lex", the welfare and safety of the People is the supreme Law: and therefore where this end is by the Trustees perverted or neglected, the People by the Law of Nature have power to preserve and secure themselves.'[2] Their *Agreement of the People* of October 1647 was an attempt to translate this contractual theory into practical politics. The *Agreement* contained proposals for a reorganization of the political, social, and legal systems and was signed by thousands of Englishmen in order to demonstrate the genuine popular consent for the proposals.[3]

At this stage the Levellers looked to Cromwell and the army for support; indeed John Lilburne, one of the leading Levellers, appealed to Cromwell as the 'most absolute single hearted great man in *England*, untainted or biased with ends of your owne' to save the liberties of all Englishmen.[4] But the Putney debates, the rejection of the *Agreement*, and the subsequent actions of Cromwell against the Levellers demonstrated the futility of relying upon Cromwell. By 1648 Lilburne was denouncing Cromwell as the 'professed enemy to the fundamentall lawes and liberties' and calling upon him to 'doe the worst thou canst to me, a man in some sense almost devoured by the Tyranny of thy fellow grand Tyrants'.[5] This remark is typical of John Lilburne, who used his own personal complaints against the political, social, and judicial systems as an illustration of the widespread popular discontent and hardship.

Lilburne continually and proudly declared his rights as a free-born Englishman:

---

[1] J. Lilburne, *Jonah's Cry out of the Whales Belly* (1647), 3.

[2] *Plain Truth*, 15.

[3] For details of this and subsequent *Agreements* see D. M. Wolfe, *Leveller Manifestoes of the Puritan Revolution* (New York, 1944).

[4] *Jonah's Cry*, 2.

[5] *The Peoples Prerogative and Priviledges asserted and vindicated . . . being a collection of the marrow and soule of Magna Carta* (1648), 57.

I am a freeman, yea a free-borne Denizen of England . . . and by vertue of being a free-man, I conceive I have as true a right to all the privileges that doe belong to a free-man, as the greatest man in England, whatsoever he be . . . and the ground and foundation of my Freedome, I build upon the Grand Charter of England.[1]

More significant than his egotism, however, is the fact that Lilburne taught others to defy tyranny and to turn to Magna Carta 'the Englishman's legall birthright and inheritance'.[2] William Prynne reported that: 'this *upstart monstrous Lawyer* since he was called to the Barre at *Newgate*, where he now practiceth, hath the *Book of Statutes* there lying open before him, which he reads and interprets to all the poore *ignorant people* that visit him.'[3] Lilburne, in fact, very successfully induced the English people to see in him the reflection of themselves, and projected individual tyrannies into pervasive social oppressions. He suffered frequently at the hands of the Long Parliament and the judiciary, and he related his hardships in the popular press, using vivid and colourful language. In one pamphlet he tells of his arrest on 19 January 1648:

that mercinary Turkish Ianisary, Col. *Baxster*, laid violent hands upon me . . . and caused his Soldiers to draw their swords upon me, and in halling of me away by force and violence, he stabbed *Magna Carta*, and the Petition of Right, etc., to the very heart and soule, and did as much as in him lyes, by that act destroy all our Lawes and liberties.[4]

By such means Lilburne and the Levellers exposed abuses in the legal system, and they based their arguments upon Magna Carta. Imprisonment without trial was declared contrary to the principles enunciated in clause 29 of the Charter, the clause of which the anonymous author of *Vox Plebis* commented 'in these few words lie couched the liberty of the whole *English Nation* . . . the perfect badge of liberty by our lawes'.[5] Gradually, however, as Leveller demands became more specific and also more radical, the Charter lost its relevance as a precedent;

---

[1] *Copy of a Letter*, 2.   [2] *The Freemans Freedom Vindicated* (1646), 6.
[3] *Lyar Confounded* (1645), 22.   [4] *The Peoples Prerogative*, Proeme.
[5] pp. 10–11.

history had now to be abandoned in favour of abstract theories of natural law.

Some of the Levellers, notably William Walwyn, had always been critical of the Charter. In *England's Lamentable Slavery* Walwyn condemned Lilburne's excessive veneration for the Great Charter, reminding him of its limitations and inadequacies; as he said, 'MAGNA CHARTA ... is but a part of the peoples rights and liberties, being . . . so little as less could not be granted with any pretence of freedom.' He challenged Lilburne to look into the past work of 'miserable Parliaments' and predicted:

> wee shall not find one Statute made to the enlargement of that streight bounds, deceitfully and improperlie called MAGNA CHARTA (indeed so called to blind the people) but if you shall observe and marke with your pen, every particular Statute made to the abridgement of MAGNA CHARTA, you would make a very blotted booke, if you left any part unblotted.

He pointed out that the Charter guaranteed the privileges of the episcopacy, 'a thing disputable and uncertain [which] was alwaies burthensome to the people'; surely, he argued, such clauses cannot be fundamental and unalterable? How then can Lilburne claim that the Charter is the 'birthright, the great inheritance of the People'? How can he revere a Charter which upholds the privileges of the oppressors of the people? According to Walwyn, 'reason, sense and the common law of equity and justice' ought to be revered rather than Magna Carta, which he dismissed as 'that messe of pottage'. He sadly reflected:

> when so choice a People . . . shall insist upon such inferior things, neglecting greater matters, and be so unskilfull in the nature of common and just freedom as to call bondage libertie, and the grants of Conquerors their Birthrights, no marvaile such a people make so little use of the greatest advantages; and when they might have made a newer and better Charter, have falne to patching the old.[1]

---

[1] (1645), W. Haller, *Tracts on Liberty in the Puritan Revolution, 1638–1647* (New York, 1934), iii. 313–16.

The Leveller weekly newspaper, *The Moderate*, at times expressed similar critical views of the Charter. In April 1649 it condemned the laws of England as 'unjust, because founded upon a rotten *Basis*', the grants of tyrannical conquerors. Magna Carta, far from being the foundation of English liberty was a reduction of that liberty and had long 'deluded' the English people: 'with this, they thought themselves in a good condition, but (poor souls) in a worse than ever; having relinquished all claim of right to the Liberties, the Freedoms demanded, and accepted the same as the Tyrants grace and favor.'[1] Such comments reflect the influence of Walwyn upon the Leveller movement, for he alone among its leaders consistently and clearly rejected the Charter in favour of abstract rights.

Richard Overton, another leading Leveller pamphleteer, could be as critical of the appeal to past precedent as Walwyn. In his *Remonstrance* he declared that 'whatever our Forefathers were; or whatever they did or suffered, or were enforced to yeeld unto: we are the men of the present age, and ought to be absolutely free from all kindes of exorbitancies, molestations or *Arbitrary Power*'. He dismissed the laws of England as 'unworthy a *Free-People*' and said that they 'deserve from first to last, to be . . . reduced to an agreement with common *equity* and *right reason*'.[2] In this work, written in 1646, Overton replaced Magna Carta by abstract natural law and innate reason. Yet the following year, in his *Commons Complaint*, he described how he, his wife, and his brother were forcibly imprisoned by order of the House of Lords and brutally treated because of their 'vindication and defence of the Great Charter'. Overton relates his spectacular journey to Newgate gaol, dragged 'by the head and shoulders . . . as if I had been a dead Dog', clutching in his hands Coke's *Second Institute* 'upon Magna Carta'. He describes in dramatic terms his fight to retain the Charter:

[1] No. 39, 3–10 April 1649. See also no. 17, 31 October–7 November 1648.
[2] *A Remonstrance of many thousand citizens* (1646), Wolfe, *Leveller Manifestoes*, 114 and 124.

I clapped it in my Armes, and I laid my self upon my belly, but by force, they violently turned me upon my back then Briscoe . . . smote me with his fist, to make me let go my hold, whereupon as loud as I could, I cryed out, murther, murther, murther. And thus by an assault they got the great Charter of *Englands Liberties and Freedoms* from me; which I laboured to the utmost of power in me to preserve and defend, and ever to the death shall maintain.[1]

Overton was variable in his attitude towards fundamental law and the Charter; indeed he could be inconsistent within the scope of a single work. In his *Appeale from the Commons to the Free People of England* he admitted the lack of precedent for such an appeal, yet he did not feel himself limited by this lack of historical support for 'Reason hath no president, for Reason is the fountaine of all just presidents'. Yet later in this work, which is a bitter condemnation of the Long Parliament, Overton called attention to their burning of petitions, an act which he called 'the highest kind of tyranny in the world', comparable to burning the Great Charter:

Oh ye free Commoners of England . . . what is become of your Lawes and libertyes: thus would they doe with *your persons*, even *burne them* by the *hand of the Common hangman*, . . . and virtually they have don noe lesse for essentially and really they have burnt the *Great Charter of England*, for in those petitions were contained the cheifest heads of that *Charter*, by virtue whereof you *hold your very lives, liberties and goods*.

He then went on to make a passionate plea for resistance in defence of Magna Carta.[2] Overton, in fact, was reluctant to break entirely with the past, and wherever possible he based his argument upon precedent; only when precedent failed to provide sufficient support for his claims did he turn to the wider, but more revolutionary, field of abstract reason.

Lilburne showed a similar reluctance to abandon the Great Charter, especially clause 29 which he regarded as 'the principal Earthly preserver and safeguard of my life, liberty and

[1] Haller, *Tracts on Liberty*, iii. 385–6 and 393.
[2] (1647), Wolfe, *Leveller Manifestoes*, 158, 171, and 173.

property'.[1] Yet Lilburne recognized that the Charter was not as comprehensive in its liberties as he would have liked. In *The Peoples Prerogative* he printed the statutes which concerned the liberties of his fellow Englishmen, but he added the proviso that the freedoms given in these statutes, from Magna Carta onwards, 'are very slender and short to what by nature and reason they ought to be'. However, he blamed this situation not upon the law itself but upon corrupt judges who 'rather serve the will and lust of the king . . . than the rules of either law, equity, reason, conscience or justice'.[2] Lilburne attempted to explain the discrepancy between the limited provisions of the Charter and the far-reaching, revolutionary demands of the Levellers by a pseudo-historical argument derived from Coke. He went beyond Magna Carta and eulogized the Anglo-Saxon past as a time when Englishmen had enjoyed all their rights and liberties freely and equally, before the arbitrary rule of the Normans. He came to regard the Charter as a partial mitigation of this Norman slavery, a 'gallant law' but which fell short of the good old laws of Edward the Confessor.[3]

There is thus a certain amount of confusion amongst the Levellers over the value of Magna Carta. Such confusion suggests that the use of the Charter by some Leveller writers was merely an attempt to guard against the charge of innovation by an appeal to history and precedent, however tortuous this might be. Their attempt was, predictably, unsuccessful; they were attacked from all sides as subverters of the historic law and constitution of England.

To Ireton, the Leveller theory of popular sovereignty could only lead to anarchy and the destruction of all government and property: 'When I heare men speake of laying aside all Engagements to [consider only] that wild or vast notion of what in every man's conception is just or unjust, I am afraid and doe tremble at the boundlesse and endlesse consequences of it.'[4]

[1] *A Remonstrance of Lieut. Col. John Lilburne* (1652), 5.
[2] Op. cit. 4–5.
[3] *A Just Mans Justification* (1647), 16 and 17.
[4] *Clarke Papers*, i. 264.

Thomas Edwards, in a bitter and scathing attack upon the Levellers, paradoxically condemned them especially for attempting to destroy the Charter, or as he put it, having 'inveighed against all Lawes from first to last, both Common and Statute, yea against Magna Carta itselfe'.[1] The ambivalent attitude of the Levellers towards the Charter is attributable partly to this constant accusation of anarchical subversion, to the need to make the past justify a programme which seemed innovative, and partly to the general assumptions of the age to which they belonged, and which were difficult to discard. Magna Carta was seen as the embodiment of the common law in opposition to the prerogative, and of immemorial fundamental law when the common law failed them; it was the safeguard of the rights and liberties of all Englishmen in opposition to king and parliament, but yet a mere 'messe of pottage' compared with the universal law of equity; it was at once a symbol of Norman tyranny and a weapon to be used against the neo-Norman tyranny of their own day. All these contradictory uses of the Charter are to be found side by side in the writings of the Levellers. But what is perhaps more striking and significant is the obvious influence which the Charter had established upon their political thought. Although confused in their interpretation of the exact significance of the Charter, the Levellers were convinced that it was of supreme significance. They all cite the Charter extensively and repeatedly, and it is rare to find a Leveller tract which is devoid of any reference to Magna Carta. Lilburne, especially, could never refrain from drawing upon his treasured Charter in defence of his conglomeration of rights. The Levellers, in fact, appropriated Magna Carta to their own ends; it was both a bible and a sword in their endeavour to restore lost liberties, a document which could be interpreted to illustrate almost any argument, and a weapon of great force in the bitter struggle against arbitrary government.

The more radical Diggers had fewer qualms in rejecting

[1] *Gangraena* (1646), iii. 216 and 217.

Magna Carta and the common law. Gerrard Winstanley demanded the complete abolition of all laws made since the Norman Conquest and the restoration of the 'laws of righteousness'. Magna Carta, to Winstanley, was an example of royal grace, and in any case it secured only the rights and liberties of a small minority of the English people.[1] In his *Appeal to the House of Commons*, he declared:

the best lawes that England hath, [viz. Magna Carta] were got by our Forefathers importunate petitioning unto the kings that still were their Task-masters; and yet these best laws are yoaks and manicles, tying one sort of people to be slaves to another; Clergy and Gentry have got their freedom, but the common people still are, and have been left servants to work for them.[2]

Yet in his troubles with the judiciary Winstanley, like Lilburne, made use of the Great Charter. But whereas Lilburne cited the Charter as his freeborn inheritance, Winstanley used it to show that the courts' judgements were contrary to their own law:

You have granted a judgment against me, and are proceeding to an execution, and this is contrary likewise to your own Laws, which say that no plaint ought to be received, or judgment passed, till the cause be heard, and witnesses present, to testifie the plaint to be true, as Sir Edward Cook, 2. part of Institutes upon 29 chap. of Magna Carta.[3]

Magna Carta, although occasionally useful to Winstanley, was merely a 'line of freedome' inserted into the law,[4] obtained after great hardship, and applicable only to a select few. It was no native right for the common people.

During the 1640s and 1650s, there was a growing realization that the law, including the Great Charter, was an inadequate safeguard of individual liberty against naked force. John Lilburne took issue with Hugh Peters for insisting that law was

---

[1] *A Letter to Lord Fairfax* (1649), G. H. Sabine, *Works of Gerrard Winstanley* (New York, 1941), 286–8.
[2] (1649), ibid. 303.
[3] *Watchword to the City of London* (1649), ibid. 322.
[4] *The Law of Freedom* (1652), ibid. 586.

nothing but the effect of force; Peters declared, 'There is no Law in this Nation, but the Sword, and what it gives; neither was there any Law or Government in the world, but what the Sword gave and set up.'[1] Yet events showed the truth of Peters's statement. Oliver Cromwell and the army held real power, and Cromwell had little regard for the law in practice, although he paid lip-service to fundamental law. In 1654 he informed the First Protectorate Parliament that 'in every government there must be somewhat fundamental, somewhat like a *Magna Charta*, that should be standing and be unalterable'.[2] Yet his true attitude to law can be seen in his treatment of political critics, and especially in the Cony case of 1655.

George Cony was a London merchant who challenged Cromwell's right to levy taxes without parliamentary sanction. He was subsequently imprisoned and sued for a writ of habeas corpus on grounds of the illegality of both his commitment and the imposition. His common law case was strong and the judges seemed about to decide in his favour when Cromwell intervened. When the judges complained and cited Magna Carta, Cromwell reminded them that he gave them their authority, and informed them that 'their *Magna F*—— should not controle his Actions'.[3]

The old belief in law as immemorial custom binding upon government was also challenged on a theoretical level at this time. Robert Filmer argued that all law is the expression of will and declared, 'there can be no laws without a supreme power to command or make them'. But he also insisted that monarchy is the only legally constituted and divinely ordained authority in society, and thus law is the command of the king, who is himself above the law.[4] The most complete enunciation and

[1] *A Discourse betwixt John Lilburne and Hugh Peters* (1649), 5.
[2] T. Carlyle, *The Letters and Speeches of Oliver Cromwell*, ed. S. C. Lomas (1904), ii. 381.
[3] Clarendon, *History of the Rebellion* (1707), iii. 650. Chief Justice Rolle resigned as a result of this blatant contempt of law by Cromwell (Campbell, *Lives of the Chief Justices of England* (3rd edn., 1874), i. 432–3).
[4] *Patriarcha and other political works*, ed. P. Laslett (Oxford, 1949), 105. See also pp. 110 and 121.

justification of this new authoritarian interpretation of law is to be found in the works of Thomas Hobbes. Hobbes insisted that law is the command of the sovereign, 'law, properly, is the word of him, that by right hath command over others',[1] and customary law has validity only as long as the sovereign allows; he wrote 'when long use obtaineth the authority of a law, it is not the length of time that maketh the authority, but the will of the sovereign signified by his silence'.[2] This is a significant change in attitude from the emphasis upon law which is clearly evident in the writings of Coke or indeed of John Lilburne, who maintained:

I know of nothing that makes a man a Magistrate over me but law, and while he walkes by the rules of that Law which make him a Magistrate, I shall own him as a Magistrate, but when he tramples it under his feet and walkes by the law of his own will, I for my part in such a condition cannot own him for a Magistrate.[3]

However, the experience of the Interregnum convinced the English of the dangers of rejecting the old theory of a balanced monarchical system of government, and the Restoration of 1660 was a reassertion of the sovereignty of law. It was a triumph for the common law as adapted by Coke over arbitrary interference from the crown, the radical claims of parliament, and the popular zeal of the Levellers and Diggers. Above all, it was a triumph for the belief in Magna Carta, 'made' as John Lilburne succinctly declared 'to keep the Beame right betwixt SOVEREIGNTY and SUBJECTION'.[4]

---

[1] *Leviathan, English Works*, ed. W. Molesworth (1839–45), iii. 147.
[2] Ibid. iii. 252. See also Hobbes's remarks on Cromwell in *Dialogue . . . of the Common Laws*, ibid., vi. 18.
[3] *The Prisoners Plea* (1648), unpaginated.
[4] *Regall Tyrannie Discovered* (1647), 20.

3

The Conflict Continued

> Then let us chear, this merry new year,
> For *Charles* shall wear the crown;
> 'Tis a damn'd Cause, that damns the laws,
> And turns all upside down.

THIS last verse of Marchamont Nedham's *Short History of the English Rebellion*[1] expresses the general enthusiasm for the restored monarchy; the overwhelming desire of all Englishmen was to return to their old constitution and the rule of law. In August 1660 the Speaker of the Convention Parliament informed the king that in order to perpetuate the memory of the liberation of the nation after two decades of anarchy and oppression: 'Your people . . . have laid it up amongst their choicest jewels, and annexed it to their Magna Charta; which they are willing to pawn unto your majesty, upon condition, when they forget this, to forfeit that and all.'[2] Such an action would have aroused a violent outcry only a few years before; but in 1660 the 'pawning' of Magna Carta seemed a small price to pay for peace and stability. In his speech at the dissolution of this parliament, the Speaker again referred to the Great Charter and thanked Charles 'for restoring us to our Magna Charta liberties, having taken the charge and care of them into your own heart, which is our greatest security, and more than a thousand confirmations'.[3] In reply, the new king expressed

---

[1] (1661), *Harl. Misc.* ii. 533. Marchamont Nedham (1620–78) was a journalist who began life as a parliamentarian; he supported the royalist cause in the late forties, the Protectorate in the fifties, and changed sides yet again in 1660. For further details, see *D.N.B.*

[2] *P.H.* 4 (1660–88), 111.

[3] Ibid. 168.

his respect for law and the Charter when, promising to observe the Act of Indemnity, he declared, 'if any person should ever have the boldness to attempt to persuade me to the contrary, he will find such an acceptation from me as he would have who should persuade me to burn Magna Charta, cancel all the old laws, and to erect a new government after my own invention and appetite'.[1]

Yet this extreme cordiality between king and parliament, amounting to subservience on the part of parliament, could not, in the light of the past twenty years, be expected to last. The old issues remained unsettled, for, although the Restoration was essentially a vindication of the concept of a legally limited monarchy, there still remained the practical problems of the extent and nature of this limitation. The crown retained extensive prerogative powers, and parliament continued to use its traditional powers in an attempt to control the prerogative. The conflict between these two basically divergent interests was quickly resumed, and appeals to history and the search for precedents by both factions brought Magna Carta once more into the centre of the debate.

The Commons used their power of impeachment against royal officials in an attempt to restrict the executive power of the crown, and the charge of contravening the Great Charter was frequently used.[2] However, the Commons' zeal in pressing impeachments aroused the opposition of the royalist House of Lords and led to a dispute between the two houses in which each appealed, albeit somewhat vaguely, to the Charter. The dispute began in 1667 when the Lords refused to commit Lord Clarendon on the Commons' impeachment because they argued that to do so would make them 'executors of process or orders' rather than judges, and that 'such a course of proceedings would not leave it in the power of the house of peers to preserve Magna Charta . . . from invasion'.[3] This aroused the

---

[1] Ibid. 169–70.
[2] For example, the Mordaunt case, *S.T.* vi. 785 ff., and *P.H.* 4, 348 ff.
[3] *P.H.* 4, 390.

fury of the Commons and, according to Cobbett, led to several 'warm speeches' on the subject of the Charter.[1] However, in the midst of the quarrel, Clarendon fled to the Continent and the matter was dropped, only to be revived in 1678 when the Commons impeached Lord Danby. The Lords again refused to commit, this time on the grounds that the offences enumerated in the Articles did not amount to treason, and the deadlock between Lords and Commons was only broken by Charles dissolving parliament.

Three years later conflict broke out over the Fitzharris case. Edward Fitzharris was an Irish informer employed by the crown. He was impeached by the whig-dominated Commons, ostensibly for writing a libellous tract against the crown, but in fact the Commons hoped that if they then promised to drop the case, he would disclose information which they could use against the crown. In the anonymous tract which the Commons claimed to be the work of Fitzharris, Charles and James were accused of being in league with France and the Papacy to impose Catholicism and arbitrary government, while 'the parliament, Magna Charta and liberty of the subject, are as heavy yokes, which they would cast off'. The author called upon Englishmen to resist such endeavours by arms if necessary: 'trust to your swords, in defence of your lives, laws, religion, and properties, like the stout earl of old, who told a king, that if he could not be defended by Magna Charta, he would be relieved by Longa Spada'.[2] However, the Commons' impeachment of Fitzharris was rejected by the Lords, who ruled that he must be proceeded against at common law, and there then followed a protracted argument over jurisdiction between the two houses. The Commons, provoked by the Lords' ruling, asserted their 'undoubted right' to impeach, and

---

[1] P.H. 4, 391.

[2] The True Englishman speaking Plain English (1681), ibid., App. xiii. This is a rather curious story; it would appear to confuse William de Longespée (d. 1236) with Earl Warenne who is said to have reached for his sword as warranty during the Quo Warranto inquiries of Edward I; see D. W. Sutherland, Quo Warranto Proceedings in the reign of Edward I, 1278–1294 (Oxford, 1963), 83 n. I am grateful to Professor J. C. Holt and Dr. G. H. Martin for advice on this point.

a number of peers agreed with them, quoting clause 29 of Magna Carta in support of this claim: 'in all ages it hath been an undoubted right of the Commons to impeach before the lords any subject . . . our law saith, in the person of the king, "Nulli negabimus justitiam"; . . . yet here . . . justice is denied to the whole body of the people.'[1] In the Commons, Sir William Jones also quoted the Charter as a valid precedent, although on rather different grounds. He declared: 'I find that it is the undeniable right of the commons to bring Impeachments in parliament . . . and that Magna Charta says not only that Subjects shall be tried "per judicium parium suorum", but "per legem terrae". And Trial in Parliament is lex terrae.'[2] Sir William developed his views in *A Just and Modest Vindication of the Proceedings of the Two Last Parliaments of King Charles II*,[3] and Magna Carta figured prominently in his argument throughout. He concluded: 'It is the commons who have reason to cite Magna Charta upon this occasion.' The imprecise language of the Charter only served to exacerbate the quarrel and provided no solution; once more the king made use of his power of dissolution to end the dispute, and incidentally to rid himself of an excessively whig parliament.[4]

As well as attempting to hinder royal policy by means of impeachment, the Commons also tried to limit the legal influence of the crown. Unrest and dissatisfaction grew over the administration of the law and the royalist bias of many judges, and the Commons tried to remedy matters by taking action against a number of individual judges who were known to manipulate the law in the crown's favour. In 1667 Lord Chief Justice Keeling aroused the wrath of the Commons by fining a grand jury of Somerset and forcing them to return a verdict of murder rather than manslaughter; when one of the jury referred to the Charter in protest, he replied, 'Magna Farta,

[1] *P.H.* 4, 1336-7.
[2] Ibid. 1338.
[3] Ibid., App. xv.
[4] Fitzharris was then indicted before King's Bench for treason, found guilty, and executed in July 1681; see *Tryal and Condemnation of Fitzharris* (1681).

what ado with this have we?'[1] The Commons intervened and accused Keeling of having 'vilified' the Great Charter, thereby endangering the liberties of the people.[2] In Keeling's defence it was argued: '*Magna Charta* he slighted not, but as being urged impertinently, nothing to the business . . . Desires it may be remembered what he has done and suffered for Magna Carta, and that his former life may be put into the balance with his present offence.'[3] This, however, did not satisfy the Commons, and two days later Keeling appeared in person before the House and made a public apology.[4] This, and the intercession of the King's Bench lawyers on his behalf, led the Commons to drop the case.[5] Yet the aggressive attitude of the Commons did not go unnoticed, for Samuel Pepys remarked on the similarity of the language between the Commons of 1667 and 1640.[6]

In 1681 the activities of Lord Chief Justice Scroggs aroused the bitter condemnation of the Commons. Scroggs was even more notorious than Keeling; he owed his appointment to the favour of Danby and aroused widespread hatred by his unnecessary severity and unlawful actions during the Popish Plot trials.[7] In 1680 he summarily discharged a grand jury of Middlesex in order to prevent an attempt to indict the Duke of

---

[1] A. Grey, *Debates of the House of Commons, 1667–1694* (1769), i. 63. Keeling's appointment in 1665 over the head of Matthew Hale had produced vociferous opposition; see Campbell, *Lives of the Chief Justices*, i. 507–8. But Keeling was free from any suspicion of republicanism, whereas Hale had served under Cromwell.

[2] Grey, op. cit. i. 62–3. See also *S.T.* vi. 992 ff. This was, of course, no new 'vilification' of the Charter; see above, p. 24.

[3] Grey, op. cit. i. 64. This remark is rather puzzling as nothing is known of Keeling's career before October 1660, when he appears at the discussions prior to the trial of the regicides. Yet on his appointment as Puisne Judge of King's Bench in 1663, Clarendon referred to his 'great Ability and Sufferings' for the king, and in reply Keeling spoke of his 'twenty years silence' (1 *Keble*, 526–7). See also E. Foss, *Judges of England* (1848–64), vii. 137 ff.

[4] Grey, op. cit. i. 67.

[5] In 1670 Keeling had to make a public apology in the House of Lords for his rudeness to Lord Holles in King's Bench (Foss, op. cit. 137 ff.) Despite his troubles with parliament, Holdsworth regards him as a 'competent lawyer' (*History of English Law* (1922–66), vi. 501).

[6] *Diary of Samuel Pepys* (1906), 592.

[7] He was charged before King in Council for browbeating witnesses but acquitted (Campbell, op. cit. ii. 18).

York as a recusant. This action was denounced in the Exclusionist Parliament, where Sir Francis Winnington warned of the dangers of such action:

we are come to the old times again, when the Judges pretended they had a rule of government, as well as a rule of law . . . If they did never read Magna Charta, I think they are not fit to be Judges, if they had read Magna Charta, and do thus so contrary, they deserve a severe chastisement.[1]

Mr. Powle agreed that any judge who had not read Magna Carta was unfit to sit on the bench, but then added 'and if they have, I had almost said, they deserve to lose their heads'.[2] The Commons proceeded to impeach Scroggs for high treason on the charge of attempting to 'subvert the fundamental laws, and the established Religion and government' of England.[3]

These two cases clearly show that both the royalists and their opponents were prepared to use the courts as a political arena and were fully conscious of the importance of controlling the law. On the whole, royal domination of the law courts remained intact, although the Commons did succeed in limiting arbitrary imprisonment by the crown. In 1679 a Commons' Bill 'for the better securing the liberty of the subject and for prevention of imprisonment beyond the seas' was narrowly passed by the Lords.[4] This Act, which is better known as the Habeas Corpus Act, gave the subject legal redress against the arbitrary power of imprisonment by the crown and provided statutory authority for Coke's definition of the writ of habeas corpus. In origin, this writ was merely a means of bringing into court those in need of proceedings; its use by an individual claiming unjust imprisonment emerged only in the late 1620s, partly as

---

[1] *P.H.* 4, 1225. [2] Ibid. 1227.

[3] Ibid. 1274. See also Grey, op. cit. viii. 237. Parliament was dissolved before Scroggs could be punished, but because of his unpopularity he was removed from office by Charles. However, he received a pension of £1,500 for his service to the crown (Holdsworth, op. cit. vi. 505).

[4] It was passed on the last day of the session by 57 votes to 55, and Burnet records that this was a mistaken count; the Bill was, in fact, outvoted (*History of His Own Time* (1724), i. 485). See also H.M.C., *11th Report*, App., pt. ii. no. 163.

a result of Coke's judgements. Its statutory confirmation in 1679 was to prove a significant addition to clause 29 of the Great Charter.

Charles II's reign also saw a violent pamphlet warfare between the royalists and their opponents. Interregnum theories were revived and repeated, and a great deal of the political writing was concerned merely to refute the arguments of others rather than to construct a complete and coherent theory of politics. Royalist theory, however, did undergo a significant change after the Restoration. The older royalists such as Clarendon had believed in the sovereignty of law and in a legally limited monarchy. This line of thought was continued after the Restoration by the opposition or whig theorists, especially Petyt and Atwood, but it came under attack from the royalists.

The first major modification of the common law doctrine was made by Sir Matthew Hale who argued that while law was indeed custom, it had not remained unchanged since time immemorial but had been in a state of continual development in response to circumstances. He refuted the claim that the common law was unalterable by showing that Magna Carta itself had altered and amended earlier law : 'the Laws contained in the Great Charter of King *John*, differed much from those of King *Henry* I'.[1] Yet Hale still maintained that the crown was limited by Magna Carta which was 'not avoidable for the King's Nonage'.[2] The majority of royalist writers, however, denied such a limitation upon the crown. Following Filmer, they argued that law originated from the crown, which must, therefore, be above the law.[3] They accepted that the king was morally bound by certain sacred obligations (for example, the coronation oath) to observe the law, but they insisted that he could not lawfully be compelled by force to do so. Yet on this issue Magna Carta presented a serious obstacle to the royalists,

[1] *History of the Common Law of England* (1713), 149.
[2] Ibid. 156.
[3] For example, Nathaniel Johnston, *The Excellency of Monarchical Government* (1686).

for clause 61 of John's Charter appeared to give legal sanction to the right of resistance. One of the most interesting of royalist tracts of the Restoration, Jeremy Collier's *Vindiciae Juris Regii*,[1] is a genuine attempt to deal with the difficulties presented by this clause of the Charter.

Collier, like all the royalist pamphleteers, rejected the validity of this clause; but, unlike his contemporaries, he justified his rejection on four well-argued grounds. First, he maintained that the whole Charter was 'a plain Concession from the Crown'; second, this clause contained no deposing power but merely provided for coercive sanctions; third, these sanctions were of little validity for 'this Charter was extorted from the King in a Menacing and Military Manner . . . [and] Rebellion is a very ill bottom to found our Liberties upon'; and fourth, this clause had always been 'counted a Nullity' and had never been part of the law. Realizing that this last claim was rather controversial, Collier enumerated in an orderly and logical fashion his reasons for this assertion: first, the clause was not mentioned in the Charter of Henry III; second, Henry's Charter was an act of royal grace and not a confirmation of an earlier right, for 'the Subjects had no Title to these Liberties before'; third, the only sanctions in Henry's Charter were religious, and therefore it provides an early illustration of the doctrine of passive obedience, not of rebellion; fourth, Collier stated that John's Charter had never had any legal authority in practice; and his final argument was that even if it had once been part of the law, it no longer had any force for it had been nullified by the Militia Act of 1661, which declared the levying of war 'offensive or defensive against the King' to be unlawful.[2]

The significance of this tract is that it contains an interesting, indeed a remarkably accurate, interpretation of the Charter, which became common in royalist thinking. Collier rejected all grants forced upon the crown as illegal and invalid, and he was able to do so without completely rejecting the Charter

---

[1] (1689). Collier (1650–1726) was a non-juror who is best known for his attacks on corruption in the theatre. [2] pp. 14–16.

because he differentiated between the Charters of 1215 and 1225. In this way royalists were able to revere the traditional liberties of Magna Carta without seeming to condone the means originally used to obtain them.

Other royalist writers similarly emphasized the illegality of John's Charter. Fabian Philipps condemned the baronial action against John in 1215 and spoke of the Charter being 'wrested and enforced . . . by a mighty Army'. To Philipps, a Charter forced upon the king by rebellious subjects did not deserve 'a recommendation to posterity'.[1] By contrast, he saw the Charter of 1225 as 'given and granted [by Henry] of his own free will and accord', and was thus able to eulogize Magna Carta and the Charter of the Forest as 'excellent Laws and Liberties . . . which, like two Jewels of inestimable price in her ears, did help to bless, secure and adorn our BRITANNIA, whilst She sate upon her Promentory, viewing and guarding Her *British-Seas*'.[2]

But the most able royalist writer of this period, Robert Brady, rejected the idea of any limitations, including Magna Carta, upon the crown. He dismissed the notion of immemorial customary law by proving from manuscript evidence that the bulk of English law dated from the Norman Conquest. He rejected the so-called liberties of the English as 'nothing but the Relaxation of the rigid Feudal Tenures',[3] and returned the Charter to its feudal context. He saw it as 'only a Relaxation of the Feudal Military Law, and . . . contrived, and Granted chiefly for the ease of Military Men'.[4] Brady pointed to the fundamental weakness of the common law doctrine when he declared that Coke 'hath a fine fetch to play off the *Great*

---

[1] *The Established Government of England vindicated* . . . (1687), 7 and 722. Philipps (1610–90) was one of the most zealous advocates of the prerogative. See also Nathaniel Johnston, op. cit., for similar views on the Charters of 1215 and 1225.

[2] Op. cit. 35 and 67.

[3] *A Full and Clear Answer to a Book written by William Petit* (1681), 44. Brady (1627–1700) was Master of Caius College between 1660 and 1700 and M.P. for Cambridge University in the 1681 and 1685 Parliaments. For details of his life and his significance as a historian see J. G. A. Pocock, 'Robert Brady', 10 *Cambridge Historical Journal* (1951), 186–204.

[4] *A Complete History of England* (1685), General Preface, xxxiv.

Charter, and interpret it, *by his Modern Law, that was not then known, or heard of*'. He scornfully asked how the Charter could be declaratory of fundamental law when Coke is unable to say what that law was.[1] Brady illustrates the new critical attitude towards history which was slowly emerging at this time. He approached Magna Carta as a historical document reflecting the political, social, and economic conditions of thirteenth-century England. In doing so, he removed the Charter from its association with the common law and the common law courts, and made a major breach in the theory of an ancient fundamental law which Coke had expounded.

Yet despite Brady's work, the Cokean interpretation continued. In particular, opposition writers looked to the past for precedents, which they used indiscriminately to support their political arguments. In doing so, they interpreted the common law theory with a narrowness which is not to be found in Coke himself. They appealed to history and precedent in a quite unhistorical way, and in their efforts to refute the royalist claim that all law is derived from the crown, they carried Coke's doctrine of an immemorial law to the length of denying that it had originated by any human action or at any fixed time. Their insistence on the law's unchanging continuity led them into dangerous historical arguments. They were forced to deny that the Normans had conquered England in 1066, for to accept the Conquest was to accept royal sovereignty. William Atwood, one of the leading opposition pamphleteers, saw 1066 as a mere change of dynasty, and claimed that William himself recognized this by his acceptance of the laws of Edward the Confessor: 'The Conqueror, consenting himself with no larger a Prerogative than their last *Saxon* King possest before him, submitted to make their own Native Common Laws of *England* the Standard of his Justice, and the continuation of their Ancient Privileges the Cement of their new Allegiance.'[2]

[1] Ibid. xliii.
[2] *The Character of a Popish Successor* (1681), *State Tracts*, i. 163. Atwood (d. 1705 ?) was a barrister and a staunch upholder of the rights of parliament.

According to Atwood, William's successors confirmed the survival of Saxon law in Magna Carta and still continue to do so in their coronation oaths.

These opposition writers were also led into historical difficulties over the question of the origin of parliament. In their attempt to refute the royalist claim that parliaments were instituted by and derived their authority from the crown, they insisted on the immemorial nature of parliament. The Charter became the centre of a controversy which developed out of earlier antiquarian interest in feudal law which Brady expanded to prove that both Lords and Commons gradually evolved during the thirteenth century.[1] Once more it was William Atwood who undertook an intensive search for precedents in order to refute Brady's argument. He insisted that representatives of the Commons had been present at Runnymede, and supported his claim with supposedly historical evidence:

The Charter of *Edward* I may well be taken for an *Explication* of the Charter of King *John*, and if it were doubtful, what King *John's* Charter meant by the COMMUNE CONCILIUM REGNI, the other makes it undeniable, that no other Common Council is meant in King *John's* but such as was provided for, by the Reservation of the *Liberties*, and free *Customs* even of every Parish.

This 'commune concilium regni', according to Atwood, was a true parliament, containing Lords and Commons, and he regarded the '*Right* of coming to Parliament' as an established part of the liberties of the subject by 1215.[2] His argument is, however, extremely confused and obscure, and by this time the common law theory had become stereotyped and untenable both historically and logically.

The whig insistence on the sovereignty of law and the immemorial customary rights of the people arose out of their need to refute the high royalist argument of divine right, which

---

[1] For further details see J. G. A. Pocock, *The Ancient Constitution and the Feudal Law* (Cambridge, 1957), ch. v.

[2] *Jus Anglorum ab Antiquo* (1681), 152 and 16. This spelling of 'consilium' is an error on the part of either the printer or Atwood himself.

Lord Shaftesbury described as 'the most dangerous, destructive doctrine to our government and law, that ever was'. He saw it as an attempt to undermine the Great Charter, indeed he warned the Lords that 'if this doctrine be true, our Magna Charta is of no use, our laws are but rules amongst ourselves during the King's pleasure'.[1] Shaftesbury reiterated his concern for the Charter in his *Letter from a Person of Quality*, in which he prophesied that if the doctrine of divine right was accepted there would be no limitation upon the actions of the monarch and individual freedom would be lost for ever: 'the 8th chapter of I Samuel will prove . . . the great charter of the royal prerogative and our Magna Charta, that says "Our Kings may not take our fields, our vineyards, our corn, and our sheep", is not in force, but void and null because against Divine institution.'[2]

The clash between crown and opposition whigs, which took place in the law courts, in parliament, and in political pamphlets, was essentially a conflict over the source of sovereign power, and it reached its climax in the early eighties over the Exclusion question. During the bitter religious and political controversy which centred on James, Duke of York, both sides drew upon the Charter. Shaftesbury and his followers played upon the deep-rooted emotional fears of popery and absolutism and used the Charter as a symbol of liberty and the reformed religion. An anonymous author commented at the time on the continuing strength of these fears: 'Slavery is as great a Bugbear in *England* as *Popery*, and the People who understand *Magna Charta* and the Bible much alike, yet will dye before they will lose either.'[3]

The royalists were more specific in their use of the Charter. In an anonymous tract they argued that to exclude James from the succession would be a violation of clause 29 'that ordains none should be put by his birthright and inheritance'.[4] This

---

[1] *P.H.* 4, 798–9. [2] (1675), *P.H.* 4, App. v, lxvi.

[3] *A Relation of Two Free Conferences between Father Le Chese and Four Considerable Jesuits* (1680), *State Tracts*, i. 417.

[4] *A Seasonable Address to both Houses of Parliament concerning the Succession* (1681), *Somers*, viii. 234. Somers attributes this tract to Halifax, but H. C. Foxcroft convincingly refutes his authorship (*The Life and Letters of Sir George Savile* (1898), ii. 532).

tract denounced the Exclusionists for acting tyrannically by attempting to force their wishes upon the nation, regardless of 'the law and the known constitutions of this land'. The author contrasted the Exclusionists' arbitrary intentions with those of Charles II and asked: 'what one illegal arbitrary act has he done in his 20 years reign? Whom has he defrauded of an ox or an ass, of life or possessions? Where has he in any one instance invaded Magna Charta, our rights, properties or liberties?'[1] Another anonymous royalist writer warned of the dangers to all Englishmen in denying James his rights, for 'if the greater be thus outed, how shall the less be secured?'[2] In this instance Magna Carta provided a better precedent for the royalists than for their opponents. However, the Exclusion attempt failed not because of the inadequate precedents of the whigs, but because of their disunity and the skilful handling of the affair by Charles II. Fears of popery and arbitrary government declined in the face of the new threat of revolution from the Shaftesbury whigs.

But the old fears were quickly revived after the accession of James and especially as a result of his two Declarations of Indulgence of 1687 and 1688. These gave freedom of worship to dissenters and catholics and suspended all laws which debarred them from civil or military office. They were termed by the royalists a 'Magna Charta for Liberty of Conscience',[3] and they provoked a considerable controversy over the comparative merits of religious and civil liberties. The whigs spoke scornfully of 'the so much talked of *Magna Charta* for Liberty of Conscience', and urged the dissenters to reject James's offer and 'continue to behave themselves like Men, who, to their great Honour, have ever preferred the Love of their Country and Religion to all Dangers and favours whatsoever'. To accept such Indulgences, they argued, would involve 'buying a

[1] *Somers*, viii. 226 and 228.

[2] *England's Concern in the Case of His Royal Highness, James Duke of York* (1680), *Somers*, viii. 168.

[3] Anon., *Animadversions upon a pretended answer to Mijn Heer Fagel's Letter* (no date), *State Tracts*, ii. 358.

precarious pretended Liberty of Conscience, at the price of the Civil Liberties of their Country'.[1] Halifax, who had played an important part in defeating the Exclusion attempt, now led the opposition to James. In his *Letter to a Dissenter* he expressed the inherent and fundamental difficulty raised by these Declarations: to accept them was to accept James's prerogative right to set aside the law. Halifax warned the dissenters:

where, to rescue your selves from the Severity of one Law, you give a Blow to all the Laws, by which your Religion and Liberty are to be protected . . . you become voluntary Aggressors, and look like Counsel retained by the Prerogative against your old Friend *Magna Charta*, who hath done nothing to deserve her falling thus under your Displeasure.[2]

Magna Carta was thus once more the emotional rallying point against the combined threat of catholicism and Stuart absolutism, and the Revolution of 1688, which resulted in the fall of James II, was hailed as a triumph for the belief in both legally limited monarchy and immemorial fundamental law expressed in the Charter.

One of the reasons given by William of Orange for his intervention in English affairs was that James had attempted the 'Subversion of the Established Religion, Laws and Liberties in England', while the expulsion of the President and Fellows of Magdalen College by James was condemned by William as 'contrary to law, and to that express provision in Magna Charta, That no man shall lose life or goods but by the law of the land'.[3] Yet the intervention of William aroused fears in some quarters for the safety of the Charter and the law. One anonymous writer warned his fellow Englishmen that William's aim was to 'reduce us to the Dutch, [which] can never be well received in England, till an act be passed to abolish monarchy, episcopacy, and all the fundamental laws, established by Magna

---

[1] Anon., *Reflexions on Monsieur Fagel's Letter* (1688), *State Tracts*, ii. 341.
[2] *Complete Works*, ed. W. Raleigh (Oxford, 1912), 134–5.
[3] Declaration of October, 1688, *P.H.* 5 (1688–1702), 4 and 6.

Charta, and all succeeding parliaments ever since'.[1] Another anonymous author recommended 'a new Magna Charta' with James which would redefine the rights of both crown and subject.[2]

The Convention Parliament, which met on 22 January 1689, also expressed interest in the suggestion for a new Magna Carta, although not with James. Having declared that James had broken his contract, abdicated the government, and left the English throne vacant, the Commons turned their attention to the more difficult problems of preventing the misuse of royal power in future and settling the form of the new government. A protracted debate then followed on the question of the respective priorities of these two problems. Many members spoke of the necessity to define the exact powers of the crown before deciding who should occupy the now vacant throne. Sir William Williams reminded the Commons of the fatal consequences of the failure of the 1660 Convention Parliament to settle the constitutional issue and urged them to consider first 'the preservation of the laws of England for the future'.[3] Mr. Sacheverall suggested the abolition of all the laws made during the last twenty years,[4] while Mr. Christie was in favour of drawing up a 'new Magna Charta'.[5] Other members, although admitting the necessity for reform, were more conscious of the need to settle the government. Indeed, Mr. Pollexfen attempted to cut short what in his opinion was a pointless, futile, and positively dangerous debate by bluntly informing the House 'if you sit till all these motions are considered, we may think to make our peace with king James as well as we can, and go home'.[6]

[1] *Reflexions upon our late and present proceedings in England* (1688), Somers, x. 180.

[2] *Honesty is the best Policy* (1688), Somers, x. 213.

[3] M.P. for Beaumaris, *P.H.* 5, 53. See also the speech by Sir Richard Temple, M.P. for Buckingham, ibid. 53–4.

[4] M.P. for Heytesbury, ibid. 55.

[5] M.P. for Bedford Borough, Grey, op. cit. ix. 34. Maynard and Pollexfen both refer to this proposal, *P.H.* 5, 55 and 56.

[6] M.P. for Plimpton, ibid. 56. Pollexfen was one of five lawyers who conferred with the Lords on the method of calling a parliament in December 1688, ibid. 24. He later became Lord Chief Justice.

The danger of prolonged debate was fully recognized by the Commons, yet despite this they were determined to state their rights and liberties.[1] Thus, on 29 January, a Committee was set up 'to bring in general Heads, of such things as are absolutely necessary for securing the Laws and Liberties of the nation', with added instructions to act as quickly as possible.[2] Burnet reports that 'it was therefore thought necessary to frame this Instrument so, that it should be like a new *Magna Charta*'.[3] On 2 February their proposals were put before the Commons, who then instructed them 'to distinguish such of the General Heads as are introductory of new Laws, from those that are declaratory of ancient Rights'.[4] The latter, which we know as the Declaration of Rights, were agreed by Lords and Commons on 12 February and received legislative form in December in the Bill of Rights, properly 'an act for declaring the rights and liberties of the subject and settling the succession of the crown'.[5]

The Declaration or Bill of Rights is a clear and explicit denunciation of Stuart government and the Stuart concept of monarchy. Like Magna Carta, the Declaration is a practical document arising out of a specific crisis and in answer to an immediate problem. The parliamentarians of 1689, like the barons of 1215, neither attempted to define royal power nor to enunciate abstract principles; they merely reiterated their ancient and undoubted rights and liberties and proclaimed the sovereignty of law. In doing so they were consciously making 'our second Magna Charta'.[6] After this there would be no need to look further back than 1689 for the foundation of English liberties, for whatever the rights of parliament and the subject

---

[1] As Hampden, M.P. for Wendover, put it, they were determined 'to declare the Constitution and Rule of the government', ibid. 57.

[2] Ibid. 58; also *C.J.* x. 15. The Committee included most of those who had made specific suggestions during the debate.

[3] *History of His Own Time*, i. 822.

[4] *C.J.* x. 19.

[5] Many of the proposals for new laws received statutory enactment separately during William and Mary's reign.

[6] Bolingbroke, *On the Power of the Prince, and the Freedom of the People*, in *A Collection of Political Tracts* (1769), 246.

might have been in the past, the Revolution settled the point without doubt. Magna Carta had been superseded. Yet its eclipse was short-lived, for when the implications of the Revolution Settlement to individual liberty became obvious, the Charter once more re-emerged as an integral part of radical political thought, a weapon to be used against the new tyranny of a class-dominated sovereign parliament.

4

The Emergence of a Rival Doctrine

IN the seventeenth century Magna Carta had been closely tied to the belief in a fundamental law. During the struggle with the crown, parliament had posed and been acknowledged as the protector of that law against royal despotism. The Revolution of 1688, which concluded this long and bitter struggle, was proclaimed at the time as the triumphant culmination of the basic ideals and legal principles expressed in the Charter.

But the men responsible for drawing up the Settlement of 1689, in their determination to place lasting and effective legal restraints upon the powers of the crown, were in fact, although they did not realize it, undermining the very law which they were trying to protect. The Revolution and its Settlement determined that in future supreme power should lie in the hands, not of the crown, but of the two houses of parliament. The foundations were thus laid for the sovereignty of parliament, a doctrine diametrically opposed to any belief in fundamental law. The eighteenth century saw the gradual realization of the implications contained in the Settlement, the practical extension of parliamentary jurisdiction, and the corresponding decline of the doctrine of fundamental law. The Cokean interpretation of Magna Carta, which in the seventeenth century was attacked on historical grounds and rejected in favour of abstract natural law, received its death-blow from its former guardian, parliament. The development of a doctrine of parliamentary sovereignty has, therefore, a distinct bearing upon the fortunes of the Charter, and we must attempt to trace its gradual emergence during the course of the eighteenth century. Yet it must be noted from the outset that Magna Carta survived the attack and endured as a formidable weapon in the struggle to maintain individual liberty.

Parliament apparently remained unaware of the implications of its new position for some years after the Revolution. The Triennial Act of 1694 was an attempt by parliament to add to the store of fundamental, unalterable law and to restrict the authority of future parliaments. It declared that 'for ever hereafter' writs should be issued for the assembling of a new parliament within three years of the dissolution of the previous parliament.[1] Such language would seem to suggest that the Commons had not worked out any theory of legislative sovereignty and that they regarded parliament as limited by fundamental principles and laws. Yet in 1716 the Triennial Act was ignored and parliament extended its term of office to seven years.[2] On this occasion parliament certainly acted as though it believed itself to possess sovereignty, and Dicey regarded the Septennial Act as 'standing proof' of parliamentary sovereignty.[3] However, the most striking feature of the debates on the Septennial Bill is the remarkable persistence of the belief in a fundamental law limiting the authority of the legislature. This was expressed with force by more than thirty peers who dissented from the Bill; they maintained that 'frequent and new parliaments are required by the fundamental constitution of the kingdom' and declared the Bill to be 'an express and absolute subversion' of the constitution.[4]

In the Commons the tories strongly opposed the Bill. Mr. Shippen[5] accused parliament of exercising arbitrary and illegal power and declared that they had no authority to extend their

---

[1] 6 & 7 William and Mary, c. 2, *Statutes at Large*, iii. 570.

[2] Septennial Act, 1 George I, st. 2, c. 38.

[3] *Introduction to the Study of the Law of the Constitution* (10th edn., 1959), 48.

[4] *P.H.* 7 (1714–22), 305 and 307. Petitions flooded into parliament protesting against this 'infringement of our liberties', ibid. 309.

[5] M.P. for Newton. He was a firm supporter of the Stuart cause and a friend of Atterbury; see below, pp. 50 ff. He opposed the suspension of habeas corpus in 1716 and in the following year was committed to the Tower for a speech against king and government, *P.H.* 7, 511.

term of office beyond their elected three years. Although he was prepared to admit that under normal circumstances the legislative power of parliament was extensive, he insisted that it was not unlimited. He argued that parliament had a duty to uphold the fundamental laws of the constitution, and that 'it ought not, on any pretence whatsoever, to touch or alter those laws, which are so far admitted into the constitution, as to become essential parts of it'.[1] Mr. Hutcheson[2] stressed the contractual nature of parliamentary authority and denounced the Bill as 'the most notorious breach of the trust reposed in us'. He regarded it as 'a very dangerous step towards the undermining of that constitution which our ancestors have been so careful to preserve and thought no expense, either of blood or treasure, too much for that purpose'.[3] He absolutely rejected any notion of parliamentary sovereignty and argued that to disregard the Triennial Act would endanger the whole body of English liberties. 'May we not', he asked, 'in the same way of reasoning, give up the Habeas Corpus act, and all the other privileges and immunities, which have been obtained to the people from the crown, from the date of Magna Charta to this very day?' He went to the extent of denying the legal validity of this Bill, supposing it was accepted by the two houses, and after quoting Coke's remark that 'an act of parliament may be void in itself', declared, 'if there be any cases out of the reach of the legislature, this now before us must be admitted to be one'.[4] Hutcheson failed to convince the Commons, however, possibly because of the excessive length of his speech, and the Septennial Bill was eventually passed by a majority of more than two to one, with the tories voting against it.

[1] Ibid. 317.
[2] M.P. for Hastings, 1713–27. An independent 'Whimsical' or Hanoverian tory, he was a prominent speaker in the Commons; see G. Holmes, *British Politics in the Age of Anne* (1967), 283.
[3] This is a reference to Matthew Paris's description of the hardship involved in obtaining the Charter; it was frequently repeated by the Levellers; see *Vox Plebis*, 9; J. Lilburne, *The Freemans Freedom Vindicated*, 6, *Regall Tyrannie Discovered*, 25, and *A Just Mans Justification*, 16.
[4] *P.H.* 7, 339, 347, and 349.

Yet this is not to say that the whigs who supported the measure necessarily accepted the modern doctrine of parliamentary sovereignty. Rather they continued to honour and uphold fundamental law, despite the difficulties into which such a belief led them. In their predicament they took refuge in evasions and either denied that fundamental law was here at stake or suggested that, even if it was, this was a grave emergency which justified exceptional discretionary measures.[1] Such an attitude is far removed from a developed doctrine of sovereignty, although it is an important, if unconscious, step in that direction. Moreover, it is not necessarily incompatible with a belief in fundamental law if the latter is understood only to imply a moral obligation upon parliament to respect certain historic rights. At first sight this would seem to be far removed from the belief in fundamental and immemorial common law, declared in Magna Carta and providing a limitation upon the actions of parliament. Yet J. W. Gough has argued, with some conviction, that such a definition is not unknown in English political thought;[2] and some lawyers doubt whether there was ever, in England, any unalterable law in the sense of a law which limited the competence of parliament. According to Holdsworth, English lawyers, including Sir Edward Coke, believed in the supremacy of a law which parliament could change.[3] At this stage a further discussion of Coke's doctrine of law must be attempted.

Coke's views on the relationship between parliament and the law have been the subject of controversy since the seventeenth century and continue to give rise to widely differing interpretations.[4] Yet his beliefs were less inconsistent and

---

[1] They argued that the disturbed conditions of the time made the holding of an election a possible threat to stability (*P.H.* 7, 314).

[2] *Fundamental Law in English Constitutional History* (Oxford, 1955), chaps. 1-3.

[3] *History of the English Law*, iv. 187.

[4] According to McIlwain, Coke believed parliament to be controlled by common law (*The High Court of Parliament* (New Haven, Conn., 1910), 83). But Dicey saw Coke as one of the earliest advocates of parliamentary sovereignty (op. cit. 41 and 48). See also R. A. MacKay, 'Coke—Parliamentary Sovereignty or the Supremacy of the Law?', 22 *Michigan Law Review* (1923-4), 215-47.

contradictory than many commentators imply. Law is fundamental, to Coke, because it is reasonable, and this is why
English common law has survived and not because it is
impossible or illegal for it to be changed. Fundamental law is
thus not so much law that is unchangeable but rather law that
it is dangerous to change; as Coke put it: 'so dangerous a thing
it is to shake or alter any of the rules or fundamentall points
of the common law, which in truth are the maine pillars and
supporters of the fabric of the commonwealth'.[1] Despite his
reverence for the common law and his scorn for the 'Men of
none or very little Judgement in Law' who sit in parliament,[2]
Coke never declared Magna Carta or common law to be
beyond the reach of parliament; rather he maintained 'the
common law has no controler in any part of it, but the high
court of parliament; and if it be not abrogated or altered by
parliament, it remaines still'.[3] This seems, at first, to be incompatible with his declaration in the Bonham case that 'when
an Act of Parliament is against common right and reason, or
repugnant, or impossible to be performed, the common law
will controul it, and adjudge such Act to be void'.[4] Yet the
most recent historical and legal interpretations of this case
suggest that Coke was arguing not for the supremacy of the
common law but for wide discretionary powers of construction in the courts, so that statute law could be brought into
general conformity with common law or, in other words, with
reason.[5]

Parliament, to Coke, was the supreme law-making authority
in the state; he wrote: 'of the power and jurisdiction of the
Parliament for making of laws in proceeding by bill, it is so
transcendent and absolute, as it cannot be confined either for

---

[1] *2 Institutes*, 74.
[2] *2 Reports*, xii.
[3] *1 Institutes*, 115b.
[4] *8 Reports*, 118a. See also T. F. T. Plucknett, 'Bonham's Case and Judicial
Review', 40 *Harvard Law Review* (1926), 30 ff.
[5] Gough, op. cit. 31–40; S. E. Thorne, 'The Constitution and the Courts',
54 *L.Q.R.* (1938), 543 ff., and *Sir Edward Coke, 1552–1952* (Selden Society Lecture,
1952); R. A. MacKay, op. cit.

causes or persons within any bounds'.[1] Indeed, he accepted the final judicial power of parliament over individual liberty even to the extent of nullifying Magna Carta, as his comments on a case of attainder in the reign of Henry VIII show. In this case it was resolved that the accused could be legally attainted of high treason without being called to answer the charge; Coke commented:

> although I question not the power of the Parliament, for without question the attainder standeth of force in law . . . albeit their opinion was according to law, yet might they have made a better answer, for by the statute of *Mag. Cart.* cap. 29 . . . No man ought to be condemned without answer.[2]

In these passages Coke seems to describe the powers of parliament as if he recognized its sovereignty. Yet this must not be over-emphasized for we must remember that Coke identified the cause of parliament with the common law. Like his contemporaries, Coke regarded parliament as the protector of the law against royal despotism. To him 'parliaments and the common lawes [are] the principall meanes to keep greatnesse in order, and due subjection'.[3] He regarded Magna Carta as referring to relations between crown and subject and never suggested—indeed never imagined—that it might be applied, or need to be applied, against parliament. His often-quoted comment 'Magna Charta is such a fellow, that he will have no "Sovereign"' refers to royal sovereignty and must be interpreted in the context of the Petition of Right debate.[4] To ascribe a doctrine of parliamentary sovereignty to Coke is anachronistic. Like his contemporaries, he believed in the sovereignty of law, with parliament fulfilling a necessary but subordinate role within this.

The Cokean stress on the duties rather than the power of parliament was reinforced in the late seventeenth century by John Locke, although on different grounds from Coke. Government, to Locke, was essentially fiduciary; it was estab-

---

[1] 4 *Institutes*, 36.   [2] Ibid. 37–8.
[3] 2 *Institutes*, 626.   [4] *P.H.* 2 (1625–42), 357.

lished for an end which was the protection of the 'life, liberty and estate' of its citizens. Parliament's powers were only those which had been given up by each individual in the social contract by which society was created, and it could 'never have a right to destroy, enslave, or designedly to impoverish the Subjects' since no individual had such a right in the state of nature. Supreme power, therefore, remained in the people, who were the source of all power and to whom parliament was ultimately responsible. As Locke wrote, 'there remains still *in the People a Supreme Power* to remove or *alter the Legislative,* when they find the *Legislative* act contrary to the trust reposed in them'.[1] There was thus no place in Locke's scheme for any theory of parliamentary sovereignty.

The development of a doctrine of parliamentary sovereignty after 1689 was hampered by the intellectual background of the English, which was derived in part from Coke and in part from Locke. This can be seen in 1701 when the House of Commons was attacked for exercising arbitrary and 'almost omnipotent power' in the case of the Kentish Petition.[2] The Petition, which called upon the Commons to grant supplies for the French war, was condemned by the predominantly tory Commons as 'scandalous, insolent and seditious, tending to destroy the constitution of parliaments, and to subvert the established government of these realms', and the five Kentish gentlemen who had presented it were imprisoned by order of the Commons.[3] Such high-handed action aroused nation-wide uproar, and a number of pamphlets appeared reaffirming the liberties of the subject. One of these, Defoe's *The Legion Letter,* followed the form of the Declaration of Rights. It enumerated the many 'illegal and unwarrantable practices' of the Commons, including the imprisonment of non-members and ignoring the petitions from and betraying the trust of their 'masters', the

---

[1] *Two Treatises of Government,* ed. P. Laslett (Cambridge, 2nd edn., 1967), 341, 375, and 385.

[2] For details see a contemporary account in *P.H.* 5, App. xvii, entitled *The History of the Kentish Petition.*

[3] *P.H.* 5, 1251.

English people. There then followed a declaration of the rights and liberties of the people and a demand for certain actions, including the immediate release of the Kentish prisoners and the grant of supplies for the war. The significance of this pamphlet lies in its Lockean stress upon the sovereignty of the people and their right of resistance. Defoe declared:

if the house of commons, in breach of the Laws and Liberties of the people, do betray the trust reposed in them, and act negligently, arbitrarily and illegally; it is the undoubted Right of the People of England to call them to an account . . . and by Convention, Assembly, or Force, may proceed against them as Traitors and Betrayers of their country.

He concluded in Lilburnean language by asserting 'Englishmen are no more to be Slaves to Parliaments than to kings'.[1]

Similar arguments appeared in another pamphlet inspired by the fate of the Kentish Petition, *Jura Populi Anglicani*,[2] in which the influence of both Coke and Locke is clearly evident. Its anonymous author accused the Commons, in Cokean terms, of having 'invaded our rights contrary to Magna Charta', thereby reducing the people to 'tyrannical slavery'. He also stressed the Lockean doctrine of trusteeship and the sovereignty of the people, declaring:

the knights, citizens and burgesses, sent by the people of England, to serve in parliament, have a trust reposed in them; which if they should manifestly betray, the people, in whom the power is more perfectly and fully than in their delegates, must have a right to help and preserve themselves.

Parliament was clearly believed to be limited by the 'laws and liberties' of the people. Yet, in practice, parliament ignored such limitations and often acted in a way which aroused fears for individual rights. We have already discussed the concern engendered by the Septennial Act,[3] and the Commons' action in 1722 against Francis Atterbury, the tory Bishop of Rochester, provides another case in point.

---

[1] *P.H.* 5, 1254 and 1255–6.   [2] Ibid., App. xviii.
[3] See above, pp. 44 ff.

Atterbury was accused of treason and imprisoned in the Tower by order of the Commons, who then brought in a Bill to deprive him of his ecclesiastical offices and banish him. Atterbury reserved his defence until the Bill was sent to the Lords, on the grounds that the Commons had no jurisdiction over a member of the upper house. The Commons therefore proceeded to condemn him unheard. When the Bill came before the Lords, the Bishop of Salisbury justified the Commons' action in a remarkable speech in which he upheld the legislative sovereignty of parliament. He declared that:

no government can subsist if there be not a power in it, to change, to abrogate, to suspend or dispense with its laws, as necessity or conveniency shall require, which is what we call absolute power . . . and there is an absolute necessity, that there should be such a power as this in every country.

He went on to deny the existence of fundamental law on the grounds that 'the state of human nature is so changeable, that it does not admit of any set of unalterable laws'.[1] Such a clear statement of parliamentary sovereignty was rare, yet even Atterbury admitted the extensive legislative authority of parliament which, he said, 'hath a greater power than the sovereign legislature of the universe: for he can do nothing unjust'. But Atterbury insisted that in practice this power had always been restrained by 'the known law' and that the proceedings against him, although not strictly illegal, were contrary to accepted legal practice and destructive to the traditional constitution.[2]

Atterbury was here expressing the view held by the tories in the early eighteenth century. While accepting the theory of sovereignty and realizing its implications, the tories regarded the exercise of sovereign power as limited by the principles of the ancient constitution and the law. Jonathan Swift declared that every government possessed 'a supream, absolute, unlimited Power . . . of making Laws . . . [which] is without all Bounds; can repeal or enact at Pleasure whatever Laws it thinks

---

[1] *P.H.* 8 (1722–33), 297–8.   [2] Ibid. 387–8.

fit'. So great is the power of parliament, according to Swift, that even the hereditary succession is alterable by statute; yet, he quickly added, 'so is *Magna Charta* too . . . which is a Truth so manifest, that no Man who understands the Nature of Government, can be in doubt concerning it'.[1]

The tories accused the whigs of betraying the principles of the Charter and undermining the ancient constitution restored at the Glorious Revolution. They pursued a vigorous campaign against Walpole's methods and policies, objecting especially to his use of the 'place' system, his manipulation of elections, and his encouragement of new economic and financial expedients, all of which were reducing the independence of the Commons, thereby destroying the balance of the constitution and endangering the liberties of the English people. Bolingbroke was particularly bitter in his attacks upon Walpole. In his *Vision of Camelick* he asserted that the people of England had been reduced to abject slavery as a result of Walpole's innovating policies. In this allegorical work Bolingbroke relates the history of the Great Charter, that 'sacred Covenant' which for centuries had guaranteed freedom and justice until Walpole 'in a bluff, ruffianly Manner . . . rumpled it rudely up, and crammed it into his Pocket', silencing complaint with gold until the people are made 'ignominious Slaves'. Bolingbroke concludes the allegory by describing the day when Walpole's 'Purse of Gold' is empty, liberty is restored, and the 'radiant Volume' of Magna Carta is returned to its former position of glory.[2]

Bolingbroke devoted his energies to ending corruption and reviving the old spirit of liberty in England. In his efforts to achieve this end, and to restrain the exercise of parliamentary power, he reiterated the old pseudo-historical views of the past which had been propounded by Coke and extended by the whigs after the Restoration. Bolingbroke believed in Saxon liberties and immemorial parliaments; he minimized the effects

---

[1] *Examiner*, no. 33, *Works* (Dublin, 1741–51), v. 224–5 and 226.
[2] (1727), *Works* (1809), ii. 3–8.

of the Norman Conquest and saw the Charter as a reassertion of the 'spirit of liberty'.[1] Like Coke, he upheld the authority of parliament but insisted that its actions were limited by the constitution; he wrote 'a parliament cannot annul the constitution' and defined the constitution as 'that assemblage of laws, institutions and customs derived from certain fixed principles of reason'.[2]

The tory attack upon Walpole and his policies stimulated the whig propagandists to defend the existing regime. Because the tories based their arguments upon ancient precedents, the whigs increasingly insisted on the perfection of the constitution established at the Revolution, and declared 'the *modern Constitution* is infinitely preferable to the *ancient*'.[3] Showing familiarity with the works of Robert Brady, although not agreeing with his political principles, the whigs stressed the lack of historical evidence for many of the tory claims. The whig *Daily Gazetteer* dismissed the editor of the tory *Craftsman* as 'an historical Idiot', and reminded its readers that Magna Carta, far from being a reassertion of former liberties, was 'only an Exemption of a *Few great Proprietors* of Land from some Hardships they lay under on Account of their conditional *Tenures*'; it made no difference to the majority of the English people who 'were as much Hewers of Wood and Drawers of Water, as truly *vassals* and *Slaves* after, as before this *Great Charter*'.[4] Another whig newspaper, the *London Journal*, pointed out that the Charter had only benefited the nobility and church, and asserted that '*Magna Charta* was *Slavery*, compared with the *Liberty* we now enjoy'.[5]

In the protracted and bitter debate which took place between whig and tory the old issues of the source of liberty, the origin of parliaments, and the nature of the constitution were revived.

---

[1] *Remarks on the History of England,* ibid. 109 ff. See also *A Dissertation upon Parties,* ibid. iii. 3 ff.
[2] *A Dissertation upon Parties,* ibid. iii. 157 and 271.
[3] *Daily Gazetteer,* no. 294, 5 June 1736.
[4] Ibid. no. 30, 2 August 1735, and no. 78, 27 September 1735.
[5] No. 769, 23 March 1734.

But the inconclusive nature of the argument and the futility of the whole exercise were recognized by the *Daily Gazetteer*, which sensibly remarked 'Our Government is the same, and the *Principles* of it the same; whatever is true or false concerning the ancient Constitution'; it went on to declare 'if our Forefathers were *Free* or *Slaves*, the Revolution stands on *the same Foundation* and its *Principles* are the same; for *Principles* . . . are eternal and unchangeable, being founded in the *Nature* and *Reason* of Things'.[1] Yet, in practice the whigs increasingly stressed the form of the constitution to the exclusion of its principles, until by the middle of the eighteenth century, as Guttridge has said, 'Whiggism stood less for the principles which had produced the Glorious Revolution than for the society and political arrangements which it had inaugurated', a society whose political basis was the sovereignty of a parliament dominated by the great whig families.[2]

It was the constitutional crisis of the second half of the eighteenth century which brought into the open the divergence that had developed between the principles and practice of the constitution. After the accession of George III the authority of parliament began to be challenged by radicals at home and also, more significantly, by the American colonists. It was the latter's refusal to accept the principle of taxation by the British government which forced parliament into openly claiming complete and absolute sovereignty. The Americans based their claim that no British parliament had fiscal authority over the colonies upon both fundamental and natural law, and in reply governmental policy was justified on grounds of the unlimited power of parliament. Lord Chancellor Northington, in a speech during the debate on the repeal of the Stamp Act in 1766, declared: 'every government can arbitrarily impose

[1] No. 96, 18 October 1735. No. 6, 5 July 1735, declared that natural rights 'are the same Yesterday, to *Day*, and *for Ever*'. For further details on this controversy see I. Kramnick, *Bolingbroke and his Circle* (Cambridge, Mass., 1968) and 'Augustan Politics and English Historiography', 6 *History and Theory* (1967), 33–56.

[2] G. H. Guttridge, *English Whiggism and the American Revolution* (Berkeley, Cal., 1942), 11.

laws on all its subjects; there must be a supreme dominion in every state; whether monarchical, aristocratical, democratical, or mixed. And all the subjects of each state are bound by the laws made by government.'[1] Dr. Johnson also asserted the practical necessity of unlimited power in every state, a power 'from which there is no appeal, which admits no restrictions, which pervades the whole mass of the community . . . bounded only by physical necessity'.[2]

The underlying unanimity shown by the major political factions on the American question is indicative of the extent to which the principle of parliamentary sovereignty was now accepted in England, although there was disagreement over the details of governmental policy. Edmund Burke did not deny the authority of parliament to legislate for the colonies— he spoke of parliament's 'unlimited and illimitable nature of supreme sovereignty'[3]—but he did question the wisdom of much of the legislation. He urged parliament rather to follow the example of their predecessors and make the privileges of Magna Carta coextensive with British rule, reminding them that 'your ancestors did not churlishly sit down alone to the feast of Magna Charta. Ireland was made immediately a partaker . . . English authority and English liberty had exactly the same boundaries.'[4]

Support for the American challenge to parliament's authority came only from those Englishmen whom Guttridge terms 'political heretics',[5] the radical reformers and those like Chatham and Camden who still believed the actions of parliament to be limited by fundamental law. Lord Chatham insisted that the colonists had 'an equitable claim to the full enjoyment of the fundamental rules of the English constitution', one of which is that a man cannot be deprived of his property

---

[1] *P.H.* 16 (1765–71), 170.
[2] *Taxation no Tyranny, Works,* ed. A. Murphy (1824), xii. 190.
[3] Speech on repeal of the American Tea-Duty Bill (1774), *P.H.* 17 (1771–4), 1265.
[4] Resolution for conciliation with America (1775), *P.H.* 18 (1774–7), 511.
[5] Op. cit. 61.

without his consent.[1] Chatham regarded the Charter as 'the Bible of the English Constitution' by which all political questions ought to be determined, and in his eyes governmental action against the colonists could not be supported when tested against this 'political bible'.[2] Lord Camden similarly judged parliamentary action according to the fundamental principles of the Charter. He denounced the Declaratory Bill of 1766 as 'absolutely illegal—contrary to the fundamental laws of nature, contrary to the fundamental laws of this constitution'.[3] He refuted the prevailing theory of parliamentary omnipotence by quoting Locke's views on resistance and reminding the Commons of their position as the trustees of the people. He declared: 'when I am asked whether the legislature cannot retract charters and annul rights, if it thinks proper, and merely at its own will, I say ... it cannot, I say, it cannot. They may be lost, they may be forfeited, but they are not to be arbitrarily sported with, and wantonly violated.'[4]

But the majority of Englishmen who sympathized with the colonists did so on grounds of representation, and their cry of 'no taxation without representation' was closely linked with their efforts at home to reform parliament and make it more representative of the people.[5] James Burgh, a radical reformer who attacked the whole system of politics in England, spoke out strongly against taxing the colonies. His constitutional criticism was essentially founded upon abstract natural law, but his defence of the colonists rested firmly upon the old-fashioned common law argument, upon Magna Carta in fact. He asked: 'if the people of Britain are not to be taxed, but by parliament; ... does it not directly follow, that the colonists cannot, according to *Magna Charta*, and the bill of right, be taxed by

---

[1] Speech on the quartering of troops in North America (1774), *P.H.* 17, 1256–7.
[2] Speech during the debate on the state of the nation (1770), *P.H.* 16, 148.
[3] *P.H.* 16, 177.
[4] Speech on the Bill for restraining the trade and commerce of New England colonies (1771), *P.H.* 17, 440–1.
[5] For further details on the movement for parliamentary reform see below, pp. 63 ff.

parliament, so long as they continue unrepresented?'[1] This is not quite what the colonists themselves claimed, however, for they argued that no British parliament, however reformed and represented, had authority to tax them.[2] Yet despite their differences, the colonists and their English supporters agreed in denying the unlimited sovereign authority of parliament, and they did so on grounds of both common and natural law. Their opposition brought to the surface the doctrine of parliamentary sovereignty which had been latent since 1689. It was now openly justified on grounds of necessity of state by the majority of practising politicians and also by a leading lawyer, Sir William Blackstone.

In his *Commentaries on the Laws of England* Blackstone argued on empirical grounds for the necessity of sovereign power, declaring: 'there is and must be in all [governments] a supreme, irresistible, absolute, uncontrolled authority, in which the *jura summi imperii*, or the rights of sovereignty, reside'.[3] This sovereign power, in England, resides in parliament whose authority is omnipotent and boundless. Drawing on past parliamentary achievements, Blackstone declared: 'It can regulate or new model the succession to the crown . . . It can alter the established religion of the land . . . It can change and create afresh even the constitution of the kingdom and of parliaments themselves . . . It can, in short, do everything that is not naturally impossible.' He concluded, 'what the parliament doth, no authority upon earth can undo'.[4] In the light of such remarks modern lawyers have tended to regard Blackstone's *Commentaries* as an authoritative statement of the modern doctrine

---

[1] *Political Disquisitions* (1774), ii. 310. Camden also declared, 'taxation and representation are inseparably united; God hath joined them, no British Parliament can separate them' (*P.H.* 16, 178).

[2] See M. Beloff, *The Debate on the American Revolution* (1949), and C. F. Mullett, *Fundamental Law and the American Revolution, 1760–1776* (New York, 1933); also H. D. Hazeltine, 'The Influence of Magna Carta on American Constitutional Development', *Magna Carta Commemorative Essays*, ed. H. E. Malden (1917), 180–226. A recent scholarly work dealing with Magna Carta in American thought is A. E. Dick Howard's *The Road from Runnymede: Magna Carta and American Constitutionalism* (Charlottesville, Va., 1968).

[3] Ed. T. M. Cooley (Chicago, 3rd edn., 1884), i. 49. The work was first published in 1765.   [4] *Ibid.* i. 161.

of parliamentary sovereignty. But Blackstone, like Coke whom he frequently quoted, was convinced that parliament would never, in practice, infringe the fundamental rights of the individual. Writing in the 1760s, he had no motive for emphasizing doctrines legitimizing revolution and every motive to play them down. Revolution, to him, was a matter of mere theory for which no positive provision existed or needed to exist.[1]

Yet Blackstone retained the traditional English claim that there are certain individual rights which are, at least by reason and in practice if not in strict law, above the power of parliament. He enumerated 'three principal and primary articles' of English liberty, 'the right of personal security, the right of personal liberty and the right of private property'.[2] He then traced the historical assertions of these three liberties, beginning with the Great Charter which, he wrote, 'protected every individual of the nation in the free enjoyment of his life, his liberty and his property, unless declared to be forfeited by the judgment of his peers or the law of the land'; he commented 'which alone would have merited the title that it bears, of the *great* Charter'.[3] Thus Blackstone's interpretation of the Charter was essentially Cokean. His inability to dispense entirely with the appeal to history and his need to find precedents for his beliefs from the ancient customs of England are indicative of the continuing influence of the common law doctrine upon his thought and are incompatible with a thorough-going belief in parliamentary sovereignty. A full and complete theory of sovereignty only appeared with the rise of Utilitarianism.

[1] He criticized Locke's theory of resistance on both legalistic and practical grounds (*Commentaries on the Laws of England*, i. 162).

[2] Ibid. i. 129. These are the three legal rights which seventeenth-century politicians and writers constantly claimed as fundamental; they are also the Lockean liberties of 'life, liberty and estate'.

[3] Ibid. iv. 424. In 1759 Blackstone published an edition of Magna Carta in which he clearly differentiated between the Charter of 1215 and its reissues: *The Great Charter and the Charter of the Forest; Law Tracts*, ii (Oxford, 1762). Before the appearance of this work there had been considerable confusion over the different versions of the Charter, and Blackstone's work was of major significance for the better understanding of the Charter, see below, p. 78.

5

Parliamentary Reform and the Charter

In the seventeenth century the main danger to individual liberty had been a powerful monarchy; in the eighteenth century the threat now came from a sovereign parliament and there was a growing awareness of the need to limit the extent of parliamentary authority.

The question of parliament's powers was brought to the forefront of politics early in George III's reign by John Wilkes. In April 1763 Wilkes published a bitter attack on the new government in his paper *The North Briton*,[1] and he was subsequently arrested on a general warrant. The issue of such warrants in cases of treasonable or seditious libel was common practice, but Wilkes was a member of parliament[2] and claimed parliamentary privilege. His efforts to secure his release were deliberately publicized by Wilkes who quickly became the idol of the London populace in a manner similar to that of John Lilburne in the 1640s. Indeed the similarities between Lilburne and Wilkes are quite striking. Both succeeded in converting a fairly simple legal case into a defence of 'the rights and privileges of every *Englishman* [against] the wanton cruelties of usurped and abused power'; both gloried in being born 'in a country where the name of *vassal* is unknown, where MAGNA CHARTA is the inheritance of the subject'; and both made frequent and impassioned appeals to the Charter, 'that glorious inheritance, that distinguishing characteristic of Englishmen'. Wilkes, like Lilburne, constantly claimed that English liberties were, in his person, being invaded and violated

---

[1] This was no. 45 of *N.B.*   [2] He represented Aylesbury.

by a tyrannical executive, and equally in his own person, must be defended. He asserted:

the liberty of all peers and gentlemen, and what touches me more sensibly, that of all the middling and inferior set of people, who stand most in need of protection, is in my case . . . to be finally decided upon: a question of such importance as to determine at once, whether English liberty be a reality or a shadow.[1]

After being granted a writ of habeas corpus in May 1763, Wilkes thanked his counsel for having 'so ably and so *constitutionally* pleaded my cause, and in mine (with pleasure I say it) *the cause of liberty*'.[2] In December Wilkes was awarded damages of £1,000 for wrongful seizure of his papers,[3] but his triumph was short-lived. A month later he was expelled from the Commons after they had declared no. 45 of *The North Briton* to be 'a false, scandalous, and seditious libel',[4] and in February a writ for his arrest was issued by King's Bench, after he had been found guilty of seditious libel and also of blasphemy.[5] By this time Wilkes had fled to the Continent, and in November he was declared an outlaw by King's Bench.

However, in 1768 Wilkes returned to the forefront of English politics, appealing even more vociferously to the Great Charter, this time on behalf of the rights of electors against an arbitrary parliament. In this year Wilkes was elected by the county of Middlesex as their parliamentary representative. But the Commons expelled him from parliament and then, after two

---

[1] *N.B.* 1. i, App., 6, 7, 27, and 34.

[2] Ibid. 7. Although Wilkes owed his release to his membership of the Commons, yet from this time the legality of general warrants was in doubt. In December 1763 the procedure was denounced by Lord Camden (*Wilkes* v. *Wood* (1763), *S.T.* 19, 1544 ff.), and in April 1766 the Commons confirmed this decision.

[3] *Wilkes* v. *Wood*, op. cit. Wilkes's success encouraged another radical, Arthur Beardmore, to bring an action against the government for wrongful arrest. In 1762 Beardmore had been arrested for publishing a scandalous article concerning the Princess Dowager and Lord Bute. He had contrived to be arrested whilst teaching Magna Carta to his son, a fact which was commemorated by a popular print after he was awarded £1,000 damages in May 1764; See Plate I.

[4] *P.H.* 15 (1753–65), 1354 ff.

[5] The charge of blasphemy arose out of his *Essay on Women* (1763).

PLATE I

Arthur Beardmore teaching his son Magna Carta (1764)

PLATE II

John Wilkes (1769)

re-elections, refused to recognize him, arguing that he was not eligible for election as he was serving a twenty-two-month sentence for blasphemy and seditious libel.[1] They proceeded to declare his opponent, Luttrell, to be the duly elected member for Middlesex. This action of the Commons raised a great public outcry. Lord Camden denounced the Commons' decision as contrary to fundamental law and declared, 'the House of Commons have assumed a power, in respect of the election in point, of setting up their will against Magna Charta, the Bill of Rights, and those fundamental laws from whence the people at large derive their privileges'.[2] Wilkes himself inflated his particular grievance into an issue of national importance; he saw his struggle for recognition as a contest between the Administration and the electorate, and declared 'there is nothing personal in it. The cause is national, and of the first magnitude.'[3] He publicly proclaimed that his aim was to restore the principles of the Great Charter:

to perfect the plan of securing and guarding the liberties of the freest nation in the world, against future attacks by wicked ministers . . . which security can only be obtained by the most wholesome laws and the wisest regulations, built on the firm basis of Magna Charta, the great preserver of the lives, freedom, and property of Englishmen.[4]

By such propaganda Wilkes quickly stirred the emotions of the people of London; prints representing him defending the Charter appeared in all the print-shops and decorated political pamphlets.[5] The Common Council of London took up Wilkes's cause and sent a number of Remonstrances to the king[6] calling for the restoration of Wilkes to his rightful place in parliament.

---

[1] P.H. 16 (1765–71), 545 ff. In June 1768 he was sentenced in King's Bench to a fine of £1,000 and 22 months' imprisonment on his outstanding conviction of blasphemy and seditious libel, although his outlawry was reversed.

[2] P.H. 16, 962.   [3] N.B. 1. ii. 596.

[4] N.B. 1. i, App., 54.

[5] See Plate II. For details of the political caricature of this period see M. D. George, English Political Caricature, vol. i: To 1792 (Oxford, 1959).

[6] In March, May, July, and November 1770.

But these met with no success, and in October a suggestion was put before the Council that the only remaining 'constitutional mode' was to appoint a committee of twenty-five. The reason for this proposal, which came from Mr. Brecknock, was drawn from history: 'that this precise number formed the committee which brought King John to reason, and that no other King of England had ever *dared* to turn a deaf ear to a Petition, when presented to the Throne after that mode, which is clearly and substantially delineated in King John's Magna Charta'.[1] Brecknock's suggestion received little support in the Council, yet it is remarkable in its revolutionary potential and is indicative of the dangerous and inflammatory state of public opinion in the city at this time.[2]

During the controversy surrounding Wilkes, Magna Carta was widely used both to justify ancient rights and as a slogan calculated to stir the patriotic emotions of the populace in Wilkes's favour. By this time the Charter had become totally divorced from its historical setting and it is doubtful whether half of those who referred to it had any personal knowledge of its contents; they merely read back into it whatever political maxim or precedent they required. An anonymous governmental propagandist voiced the danger of such a situation when he wrote, '*Liberty, Constitution, Magna Charta*, the *Revolution* are Words which, if they were less frequently founded, would probably be more strongly felt, and more duly revered.' He went on to warn that 'when there is real Danger to our Liberties, we shall scarce persuade ourselves

---

[1] *N.B.* II. ii. 548. The king's rejection of the Remonstrances led Lord Chatham to draw upon the Charter in defence of the right of petitioning; in a speech in the Lords in 1770 he declared 'the subjects of this realm are not only entitled by Magna Charta and the Bill of Rights to petition, wherever they suppose themselves aggrieved, but by a variety of laws as expressive as they are numerous' (*P.H.* 16, 967).

[2] Brecknock repeated his proposal in a letter to *The North Briton* published on 10 November 1770 (*N.B.* II. ii. 553–4). The editor, Bingley, supported the idea and called for the election of national representatives who would then nominate twenty-five 'barons' to form a standing committee to redress grievances (ibid. 554). Bingley, in fact, has here turned Brecknock's original idea into a demand for a general election; see also ibid. 527–8.

that the Wolf is at the Door'.[1] Others questioned the sincerity of Wilkes's high-sounding talk of the Charter and English liberties. In 1774 Wilkes was allowed to re-enter the Commons, and by 1775, according to Horace Walpole, the 'protector' of Magna Carta was 'sick of his part': 'though he called the resolution of the last Parliament [expelling him from the Commons] a violation of Magna Charta, he said in a whisper to Lord North, he was forced to say so to please the fellows who followed him'. Walpole comments that 'this was his constant style'.[2] Modern historians tend to accept Walpole's opinion; Ian Christie sees Wilkes as deliberately courting publicity for selfish ends and dismisses him as 'a propagandist and demagogue', devoid of political principles.[3] Yet the Wilkes issue was indicative of the growing public concern outside parliament over the nature and extent of parliamentary authority. Wilkes's significance, like that of John Lilburne earlier, lay in his demagogic abilities, in the fact that he drew the attention of the people to the arbitrary tendencies of parliament and the dangers to individual liberty which this involved. Magna Carta was one of the chief weapons used by both in their self-appointed task.

The arbitrary proceedings of the executive, supported by a subservient House of Commons, against Wilkes and other radicals served to increase existing fears that the balance of the constitution was being destroyed; and a reform movement developed aimed at redressing the balance and restoring 'the original excellence of the Constitution'.[4] The practical means proposed to achieve these ends were threefold: first, the rejection of placemen from the Commons; second, shorter parliaments; and third, more equal representation. The first two points had been advocated since the reign of William III with the aim of reducing ministerial influence in the Commons and

[1] *A Defence of the Majority in the House of Commons on the Question relating to General Warrants* (1765), 43–4.

[2] *Journal of the Reign of George III*, ed. J. Doran (1859), i. 465.

[3] *Wilkes, Wyvill and Reform* (1962), 227.

[4] C. Wyvill, *Political Papers* (York, 1794–1802), ii. 220.

of preventing the development of arbitrary tendencies within the Commons.[1] The third point, however, was a new demand, characteristic of the essentially novel movements for parliamentary reform under George III.

Whatever the actual details of their proposals, the advocates of parliamentary reform maintained that their aim was not innovation but restoration, and they constantly appealed to history, especially the Charter, in support of their claim. Indeed one of the reformers, Granville Sharp, based his whole political philosophy upon the Great Charter, which he believed to be fundamental and unrepealable. Explicitly denying the doctrine of parliamentary sovereignty, Sharp asserted that no single parliament had sufficient authority to repeal the Charter. His reason for this claim was that the Charter had been confirmed by numerous parliaments and so could only be repealed by the same number, or as he wrote, 'by the same *accumulated Authority*'.[2] Such a forceful statement of the fundamental nature of the Charter was rare, however, in the eighteenth century.[3] Few of the reformers were prepared to commit themselves on this tricky question of fundamental law, although they eulogized the Charter as a restoration of the ancient liberties of Saxon England which had been destroyed in 1066. Indeed, the influential *Historical Essay on the English Constitution*[4] recommended 'a day of public thanksgiving, festivity, and joy' as an annual and perpetual reminder of England's deliverance from tyranny in 1215.[5] Many of the reformers saw themselves as the successors of the thirteenth-century barons; in December 1779

[1] See above, p. 52.

[2] *A Declaration of the People's Natural Right to a Share in the Legislature* (1774), 204. See below, p. 91.

[3] During the debate on the Declaratory Bill, Wilkes made a similar assertion when he asked the Commons, 'Can we . . . repeal Magna Charta? Has this House the power to establish the Mohometan religion?' and gave the answer 'There are fundamental inalienable rights, landmarks of the constitution, which cannot be removed' (*P.H.* 19 (1770–8), 570).

[4] Published anonymously in 1771, it was probably written by Obadiah Hulme. It was serialized in *The Patriot* and used by Cartwright in his *Take Your Choice* (1776).

[5] *The Patriot*, ii. 69.

a meeting of the Yorkshire freeholders, from which the famous County Association movement developed, was publicized as 'a second Runnymede'.[1] The reformers frequently compared the governmental system of their own day with Norman tyranny and asserted, 'it is now as expedient for the people at large to interfere as at the time when Magna Charta and the Bill of Rights were granted'.[2] In addition, they were encouraged in their demands by the activities of the American colonists whom they believed to be fighting for 'an American Magna Charta'.[3]

Yet some of the reformers were critical of the excessive veneration afforded to the Charter. As early as 1774 Major John Cartwright condemned the tendency to inflate the importance of the Charter, which he regarded as the product and not the foundation of English liberty:

That 'Magna Charta is the great foundation of English liberties, and the basis of the English constitution', I must positively deny. It is indeed a glorious member of the superstructure, but of itself would never have existed, had not the constitution already had a basis, and a firm one too.

He went on to describe the Charter as 'a mere formal declaration of rights, already known to be the constitutional inheritance of every Englishman'.[4] By 1797 Cartwright even denied that the Charter was a part of the constitution of England; it was rather a charter 'of a peculiarly sacred character . . . declaratory of the people's *rights* on certain points; thereby shewing what *in those respects* the constitution is'. He condemned the provisions of the Charter as petty and inadequate. on the

---

[1] *London Evening Post*, H. Butterfield, *George III, Lord North and the People, 1779–1780* (1949), 256.

[2] *York Chronicle*, Butterfield, op. cit., 257. The reference to the Bill of Rights derives from the fact that the reformers regarded the Convention Parliament of 1689, like the barons of 1215, as an 'association' formed to safeguard English liberties.

[3] *P.H.* 19, 536. Also see above, pp. 54 ff.

[4] *American Independence* (1774), 39.

grounds that 'not one of them related to the essentials of political liberty'. To Cartwright, the establishment of an independent and truly representative parliament was the essence of liberty, and he criticized the barons of 1215 for not having realized this 'simple' fact.[1] Cartwright advocated the 'framing of a new Magna Charta' to restore the real liberties of the English people.[2]

The growing criticism by Cartwright of the liberties contained in the Charter is illustrative of the increasing radicalism of the reformers. At the outset their demands were moderate and they were quite satisfied with the appeal to history. The success, in April 1780, of Dunning's rather vague motion that the influence of the crown ought to be diminished satisfied many, including Horace Walpole who regarded this motion as 'a codicil to Magna Charta'.[3] Yet there were more radical elements within the reform movement who were not so easily satisfied. The Westminster Committee in the eighties and the London Corresponding Society in the nineties began to formulate more specific and far-reaching demands, including universal manhood suffrage, for which it was increasingly difficult to find precedents. Like their Leveller predecessors, these radical reformers turned to abstract natural rights which many of them transposed into an idealized past.[4] The liberties of the Charter now began to be seen as narrow, partial, and inadequate when compared with the 'free and glorious Constitution' of Saxon days.[5] Yet even so, Magna Carta was not totally rejected. Members of the London Corresponding Society attacked the legal abuses of their day on grounds of clauses 14 and 29 of the

---

[1] *An Appeal on the subject of the English Constitution* (Boston, 1797), 31 and 37–8.

[2] *Letter to the Electors of Nottingham* (1803), 18.

[3] *Letters of H. Walpole*, ed. P. Toynbee (Oxford, 1903–25), xi. 155. Some years before, Walpole wrote to George Montagu that 'on each side of my bed I have hung the *Magna Charta*, and the Warrant for King Charles' execution, on which I have written *Major Charta*: as I believe, without the latter, the former by this time would be of very little importance' (ibid. iv. 1).

[4] See the Report of the Sub-Committee of the Westminster reformers, Wyvill, op. cit. i. 236, and the letter from the Sheffield Corresponding Society to that of Edinburgh, *P.H.* 31 (1794–5), App. F, no. 1, 838–9.

[5] J. Thelwall, *The Natural and Constitutional Rights of Britons* (1795), 27.

Charter. Using language similar to Granville Sharp's, they complained that:

the various methods now in constant practice by which the benefits of [clause 29] are totally defeated and destroyed, might induce us to suppose, that the Great Charter has been repealed; if we did not assuredly know, that it is the fundamental basis of our constitution; which even the real representatives of the people (much less the miserable nominees of Helstone and Old Sarum) have not the right, nor . . . the power to repeal.[1]

But the increasing radicalism of the reformers, coupled with their denunciation of the war against France, alienated many of their former supporters, aroused the fears of the political classes, and led to the repressive legislation of 1795.

The reform movement, which declined in the 1790s, was revived in the following decade under the impetus of Francis Place, John Cartwright, William Cobbett, and Sir Francis Burdett. Indeed it was Burdett's election as member of parliament for Westminster in 1807 that reopened the old debate on the composition of the Commons and the extent of parliamentary authority. Burdett, like Lilburne and Wilkes before him, brought home to the people the political issues of the day. He set himself up as the defender of the rights and liberties contained in the ancient constitution against arbitrary innovation, as the defender of the Great Charter and the birthright of all Englishmen. In 1809 Burdett proposed a 'Plan of Parliamentary Reform' in the Commons to restore 'the fair balance of the Constitution'. During his speech he announced his firm intention to 'hold fast by that plain and substantial Constitution, adapted to the contemplation of common understandings, *to be found in the Statute Book, and recognised by the Common Law of the Land*'.[2] His plan was, of course, rejected by the Commons, but a few months later Burdett achieved popular acclaim by

---

[1] *Address to the people of Great Britain and Ireland* (1794), P.H. 31, 481. See *S.T.*, vols. 24 and 25 for the trials of members of the London Corresponding Society in 1794.

[2] *P.D.* 14 (1809), 1042–3 and 1046.

denouncing the excessive and arbitrary action of the Commons against Gale Jones.

In 1810 Jones was imprisoned by the Commons for publicly questioning their proceedings in disrespectful terms.[1] Burdett declared their action to be a violation of the common law, Magna Carta, and trial by jury. He accused them of refusing to give up the 'usurped power and authority' claimed by the Long Parliament, and reminded them that they were subject to 'the law of the land and the principles of the constitution'.[2] In addition to this internal attack on the body of which he was a member, Burdett published his views in a deliberately inflammatory open letter to his constituents.[3] This is a work in the Cokean tradition, full of emotive references to the birthright and liberties of Englishmen, the law of the land, Magna Carta, and the ancient constitution. Yet despite his somewhat archaic language, Burdett was expressing a very real and urgent problem, that of defining the extent of parliamentary jurisdiction over the lives and liberties of the subject, or, as he himself put it, 'whether our liberty be still to be secured by the law of our forefathers, or be to lay at the absolute mercy of a part of our fellow-subjects'. To Burdett, the Commons' action against Jones was 'a declaration, that an Order of theirs is to be of more weight than Magna Charta and the Laws of the Land'. The whole work is a sustained and forceful condemnation of the actions of the Commons, drawing heavily on Magna Carta, and it is hardly surprising that the Commons denounced it as 'libellous and scandalous' and ordered the arrest of Burdett for breach of privilege.[4] Burdett barricaded himself into his

---

[1] Jones, who had been a leading member of the London Corresponding Society, was President of the British Forum, a reform organization. In February he placarded Westminster with a bill announcing a debate at the Forum, for which he was summoned to the bar of the Commons; despite his apology, he was imprisoned by order of the Commons.

[2] *P.D.* 16 (1810), 14 xxxx and 15 xxxx (odd pagination).

[3] *Denying the power of the House of Commons to imprison the people of England*, P.D. 16, 137–75. The letter appeared in Cobbett's *Political Register*, a radical reformist weekly.

[4] *P.D.* 16, 186.

PLATE III

The Arrest of SIR F^S. BURDETT. MP

Burdett's son holds a copy of Magna Carta as his father is arrested (1810)

PLATE IV

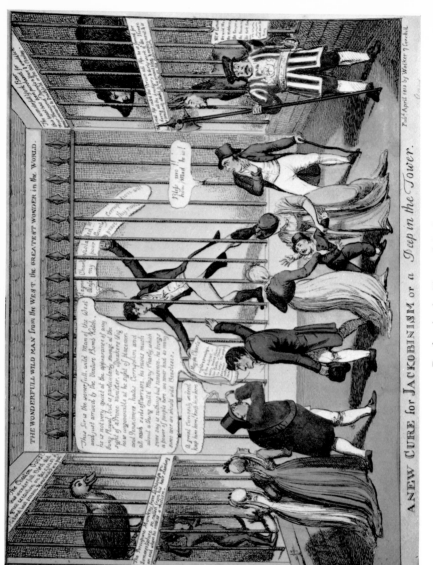

Burdett in the Tower (1810)

house and evaded arrest for four days, during which time mass demonstrations took place in the city of London in his favour. Eventually he was arrested whilst teaching his fourteen-year-old son to translate the Great Charter.[1] Popular prints of the arrest flooded the print-shops,[2] further demonstrations took place, and the Commons was bombarded with petitions demanding the release of Burdett and Jones.[3] In the Commons a proposal for 'a Magna Charta of parliament' to define the privileges of the Commons and prevent arbitrary action in future received no support.[4]

The Commons consistently denied that their action against Burdett had contravened the Charter; they claimed that the power to imprison for libel was part of the 'fundamental law of Parliament', which law was 'part of the lex terrae, mentioned in Magna Charta'.[5] They quite rightly criticized the 'general construction' put upon the Charter by Burdett and his supporters, and argued that, if carried to its logical conclusion, such an interpretation would produce a situation in which even 'canon law and the ecclesiastical law were of no authority as they are not contained in Magna Charta'.[6] In addition, it was suggested that the radicals had little knowledge of the provisions of the Charter they were so fond of quoting. Mr. Bourne suspected that 'persons talk of Magna Charta who have never read it'; he reminded the Commons that the Charter was originally a feudal document and thus many of its provisions were 'totally inapplicable to the present state of the country'. While admitting that some of its clauses retained their relevance, he pointed out that these had been confirmed by later statutes such

---

[1] A patriotic gesture earlier adopted by Arthur Beardmore, see above, p. 60 n. 3. For a fuller account of Burdett's arrest see W. Cobbett, *A History of the last hundred days of English freedom* (1820), and also M. D. George, *English Political Caricature*, vol. ii: *1793–1832* (Oxford, 1959), 125–7.

[2] See Plates III and IV.

[3] *P.D.* 16, 780, 885, and 949; *P.D.* 17 (1810), 441. Burdett was released after two months, following the prorogation of parliament. His release was the occasion for further public demonstrations and more prints; see Plate V.

[4] *P.D.* 16, 697. Proposed by Mr. Fuller, M.P. for Sussex.

[5] *P.D.* 17, App. xciii.

[6] *P.D.* 16, 986.

as the Bill of Rights. Showing a greater historical sense than the radicals, he stated that 'nothing was more absurd than to take [Magna Carta] as the standard by which we were exclusively to regulate ourselves'.[1] His remarks went unheeded, however, and the Charter and the ancient constitution continued to figure large in the reform agitation which now began to be more organized.

In 1812 the Hampden Club was formed in London and provincial subsidiaries quickly followed. Newspapers such as *The Political Register*, *The Black Dwarf*, and *The Reformer's Register* publicized demands for universal suffrage, annual parliaments, and vote by ballot. Not unnaturally, the fears of the propertied classes were revived, and in 1817 the Liverpool Government took action. Repressive legislation was justified as an attempt to maintain the traditional constitution from 'the assaults of furious and desperate men'.[2] Yet measures such as the Suspension of the Habeas Corpus Act in 1817 aroused an outcry both inside and outside parliament in defence of individual liberties. Marquess Wellesley complained that the English people had been deprived of 'their personal freedom, their birthright secured to them by Magna Charta'.[3] Sir Francis Burdett made the novel suggestion that the Habeas Corpus Act should be completely obliterated from the statute-book, for then 'the people would be left to the protection of Magna Charta, under which they had the same right of personal protection; the statute of Habeas Corpus affording only a summary remedy to persons aggrieved'.[4] On a later occasion Burdett condemned the lack of justice in England and mockingly commented that 'Magna Charta had become obsolete of late' for it was an 'old fashioned law, not suited to the refinements of modern times'.[5] Wooler published a satirical article along the same lines in *The Black Dwarf* in which he pointed out the 'bad family connexion' of Habeas Corpus, 'descended from two notorious *traitors* of

[1] M.P. for Christchurch; *P.D.* 17, 143.
[2] Speech by Canning in support of the Seditious Meetings Bill, *P.D.* 35 (1817), 638–9.
[3] Ibid. 566.   [4] *P.D.* 37 (1818), 89.   [5] Ibid. 490.

PLATE V

Burdett after his release from the Tower (1810)

old times, called *Magna Charta* and the *Bill of Rights*'. He quickly added, for the peace of mind of the government, that these two statutes were 'incapable of interfering in affairs of government', Magna Carta in particular being 'so very old and infirm that he seldom stirs abroad, and when he does he is sure to be insulted, and is very glad to get back to his lodgings again'.[1]

The reformers organized petitions to parliament in 1817 and 1818 protesting against the repressive legislation and demanding immediate reform.[2] These led Henry Brougham to speak out forcibly in the Commons against those who were attempting to 'delude [the people] with their little nostrums and big blunders to amend the British Constitution'. He reminded the Commons that little was known of the ancient constitution which the radicals revered, indeed he doubted whether the Saxons had ever had a constitution.[3] He vehemently denied that universal suffrage was 'a right for which our ancestors shed their blood', and when Burdett quoted clause 29 of the Charter to support the demand for universal suffrage, Brougham was quick to point out that this was an unfortunate precedent for the reformers as in fact it refuted the argument it was cited to prove; the inclusion of the word 'liber' clearly indicated that 'liberty was only allowed to those who had property in men, instead of being the property of men'.[4] Once again the language of the Charter helped to intensify the quarrel and offered no solution. Yet despite this, both radicals and conservatives continued to justify their conflicting views of the constitution by vague appeals to the past.

The popular agitation for radical reform which dominated the second decade of the nineteenth century, and which repressive

---

[1] No. 6, 5 March 1817, i. 95. Rudyard made a similar remark in 1628 (Rushworth, *Historical Collections*, i. 552). Wooler regarded the Charter as evidence of the spirit of freedom which had always existed amongst the English. He declared that 'it was only to exhibit to their children the means that made them free, that [our ancestors] left this memorial to after ages' (*The Black Dwarf*, no. 1, 29 January 1817, i. 1).

[2] *P.D.* 35 (1817), 643 ff.; *P.D.* 37 (1818), 217; *P.D.* 38 (1818), 1037 ff.

[3] *P.D.* 35, 365-6.

[4] *P.D.* 38, 1157. See also ibid., 1180 ff. for Burdett's reply.

legislation failed to eradicate, was reinforced in the 1820s by a more moderate reform movement which was justified by appeal to the past. Lord John Russell made a number of proposals for limited reform and declared that his aim was to reconcile the extreme radicals and the ultra-conservatives.[1] Thus on the one hand he was bitter in his condemnation of those who rejected all suggestions of reform, 'who are so wedded to the ancient constitution, that they overlook their unsuitableness to modern times, and the altered condition of society';[2] but yet he voted against radical proposals for universal suffrage and vote by ballot on the grounds that these would undermine the 'fundamentals' of the constitution which he wished to preserve.[3]

Those who opposed even moderate reform also argued on pseudo-historical grounds. They spoke of the dangers of destroying or undermining the 'balance' of a constitution which Canning, one of the most consistent and outspoken critics of reform, believed to be 'as nearly poised as human wisdom can adjust it'.[4] However, by 1830 the tide of reform was turning. The tory party, long opponents of reform, had been split over catholic emancipation,[5] while the whigs were coming to believe that a measure of moderate reform would keep England free from revolutionary activity such as occurred in France in 1830, and thus prevent the radicals from totally destroying the constitution. They therefore reluctantly supported the moderate proposals of Lord Grey's Government, whose declared aim was to 'preserve the spirit' of the constitution.[6]

---

[1] *P.D.* 41 (1819–20), 1093.

[2] *P.D.*, new series, 22 (1830), 869.

[3] *P.D.*, new series, 24 (1830), 1229.

[4] Speech at Liverpool, May 1820, *Speeches with a memoir by R. Therry* (1828), vi. 391.

[5] The question of catholic emancipation aroused great debate. The measure was attacked as destructive to the fundamental principles of the constitution and protestantism (*P.D.*, new series, 20 (1828), 879 ff.). See also *P.D.*, new series, 19 (1828), 379 for Burdett's views.

[6] Lord John Russell introducing the first Reform Bill in March 1831 (*P.D.*, 3rd series, 2 (1830–1), 1085.

During the protracted debates over the governmental proposals, both sides appealed to precedent and saw themselves
as the defenders of the 'true' principles of the constitution.
Opponents denounced the Reform Bill as 'subversive at once
of the principles of the Constitution and of every received
notion of British freedom';[1] they preferred to 'confide in the
wisdom of our ancestors than the theories of the moderns'.[2]
On the other hand, supporters of reform saw the past in a very
different light. They argued that the history of the English
constitution was one of constant change and improvement.
Mr. Gally Knight pointed out that Magna Carta itself was 'a
great innovation', and asked 'had our forefathers been guided
by the much-extolled maxim of "let things alone", where would
have been our boasted constitution?'[3] Macaulay, making a
similar point, called the Bill 'a greater charter of the liberties of
England'.[4]

But the Reform Act of 1832 satisfied very few. In particular,
the agitation which preceded it had stirred up the social and
political aspirations of a wide section of the lower classes which
the Act did nothing to satisfy. As Lovett said, it rather 'aggra-
vated the painful feeling of . . . social degradation, by adding
to it the sickening of still deferred hope'.[5] Disillusioned with
both political parties, the radicals began to press more urgently
for real reform, appealing directly to the people. *The Birmingham
Journal* declared 'that the Reform Bill may become what you
hoped it would be, a Great Charter of English Liberty, depends
on the People alone'.[6] It was out of such determination following the disappointment of the Reform Act that the Chartist
movement of the late 1830s and 1840s emerged.

Like the Levellers of the seventeenth and the parliamentary
reformers of the eighteenth centuries, the Chartists initially
justified their demands by an appeal to the past. But,
again emulating their radical predecessors, they quickly found

---

[1] Ibid. 5 (1831), 426.   [2] Ibid. 3 (1831), 216.
[3] Ibid. 4 (1831), 718.   [4] Ibid. 783; see also p. 777.
[5] *Life and Struggles* (1876), App. C, 470.
[6] A. Briggs, *Chartist Studies* (1959), 22.

precedents too limiting and were forced to abandon history in favour of more far-reaching abstract claims. The ideas and proposals contained in the People's Charter, drawn up by the London Working Men's Association in 1838, were neither original nor new; they were merely a restatement of old radical demands. However, the choice of the word 'Charter' remains something of a mystery. There is no documentary evidence to connect the People's Charter with the Great Charter, nor indeed with more recent precedents such as the French Charter of 1830 or the Belgian Chartre Constitutionelle of 1831. It seems likely that the word 'Charter' was suggested by unconscious memory rather than by inspiration, and that it covered the whole mass of immemorial liberties of Englishmen.[1]

The majority of the Chartists had an extremely unhistoric and nostalgic attitude towards the past, which they used to intensify the grievances of the present. They contrasted the evils of industrialization with a rural past in which all men enjoyed their birthright without hindrance. This myth of a lost age of liberty was a potent argument. Addressing a huge rally on Heartshead Moor in 1838, the Reverend Joseph Raynor Stephens declared 'We stand upon our rights—we seek no change—we say give us the good old laws of England unchanged'; and when he received the shout of 'Magna Charta' to his question 'What are these laws?', he replied: ' "Aye, Magna Charta! The good old laws of English freedom—free meetings—freedom of speech—freedom of worship—freedom of homesteads—free and happy firesides, and no workhouses." (Cheers)'[2]

Yet the Chartists were more concerned with the future than the past and, despite their name, they made little positive use of Magna Carta. Along with the laws of King Alfred, the Charter

---

[1] Lovett insisted that 'the principles of our charter were the laws and customs of our ancestors' (op. cit. 213); while Fergus O'Connor defended the People's Charter as the embodiment of 'the judgement of our ancestors', *Northern Star*, 28 July 1838.

[2] Place Papers, 32, B.M. Add. MS. 27820, App. K, 2.

figured occasionally in their argument, but more often they referred vaguely to the composite liberties of the past without specifying them in any way. The reasons for this appear to be threefold: first, despite Fielden's claim that 'universal suffrage is to be found in Magna Charta',[1] the Charter did not provide a precedent for any of their six demands; second, it was a much quoted 'tool' of their opponents, for politicians of both parties based their rejection of Chartist demands upon historical arguments;[2] and third, although the Charter still remained an emotive popular rallying cry against authority, as a limitation upon the actions of government it was worthless in practice, for the common law foundations of the 'myth' had been undermined not only by the development of practical parliamentary sovereignty, but also by new intellectual movements of the late eighteenth and early nineteenth centuries.

[1] Ibid.
[2] See the debate of 3 May 1842, *P.D.*, 3rd series, 63 (1842), 13 ff.

6

The Charter Attacked

THE later eighteenth century saw a number of changes in the intellectual climate of thought which had important repercussions on the persistence of the common law tradition, with its corollary emphasis on the Charter. Under the influence of ideas and events in France and America, certain English theorists began to abandon the appeal to history in favour of abstract natural law. They stressed the unlimited and inalienable rights belonging to all men and rejected the past in favour of 'reason and equity and the rights of humanity'.[1] James Mackintosh, writing in defence of the principles of the French Revolution, denounced precedent as 'feeble, fluctuating, partial and equivocal' and urged the English to cease their reverence for what he called 'this ignoble and ignominious pedigree of freedom'. He declared, 'it is not because we *have* been free, but because we have a right to be free, that we ought to demand freedom'.[2] Yet Mackintosh was unable to break away completely from the traditional assumptions of his age. He differentiated between the inadequacies of the past, in which men were only 'partially enlightened', and the principles which had endured through the ages, sensibly pointing out that 'admiration of Magna Charta does not infer any respect for villainage'.[3] Indeed some years later Mackintosh produced one of the most extreme eulogies on the Charter in the English language.[4]

Only Tom Paine succeeded in rejecting outright the historical

---

[1] Richard Price, *Observations on the Nature of Civil Liberty* (2nd edn., 1776), 32.
[2] *Vindiciae Gallicae* (1791), 305–6.
[3] Ibid. 331.
[4] *History of England* (1830), i. 222. See below, p. 107.

assumptions of his age. Unlike his contemporaries, he refused even lip-service to the past and complained of the 'superstitious reverence for ancient things' which prevented much-needed reform. He upheld the right of every generation to alter laws and institutions as the occasion demanded, declaring, 'I am contending for the rights of the *living*, and against their being willed away, and controuled and contracted for, by the manuscript authority of the dead.' He believed that the ancient charters which the English admired were, in fact, reductions of former liberties, for 'rights are inherently in all inhabitants; but charters, by annulling those rights in the majority, leave the rest, by exclusion, in the hands of a few'.[1] Magna Carta, to Paine, was certainly not the foundation of English liberty; it was rather a partial resumption of man's inherent civil liberties, 'no more than compelling the Government to renounce a part of its assumptions'.[2] Nor was the Charter irrevocable, for Paine explicitly rejected any notion of fundamental law; following Hobbes, he declared, 'a law not repealed continues in force, not because it *cannot* be repealed, but because it *is not* repealed; and the non-repealing passes for consent'.[3] Paine replaced common law and precedent by concepts of abstract law and natural rights and carried one stage further the work begun by Hobbes and Locke. But the general state of English opinion in the 1790s was very unfavourable to the spread of his ideas. The French Revolution produced a conservative reaction amongst the English, who defended with increased determination their ancient constitution and traditional ways of thought.[4]

At the same time, the 'myth' of the Charter was being quietly transformed by improvements in historical method and technique. This new movement involved a departure from both the common law tradition and the revival of natural law in its abstract form which marked the work of Paine. Writers of the Historical School regarded the state, its laws, and

---

[1] *Rights of Man* (1791), *Selected Works of Tom Paine*, ed. H. Fast (New York, 1945), 99, 218, and 235.
[2] Ibid. 215. [3] Ibid. 101. [4] See above, p. 67.

institutions as the result of a long and gradual process spread over generations. They rejected the ideas of immemorial liberties, the Saxon constitution, and other mythical notions which had by this time, if not in origin, become an integral part of the common law tradition; they looked instead to the overriding causal laws and concepts governing any particular society or period of time.[1] Indeed one of these writers, John Millar, regarded Magna Carta itself as an example of an overriding causal law. The significance of the Charter, to Millar, lay in its survival rather than in its inherent qualities. He pointed out that in origin the Charter was a limited baronial measure aimed to secure 'the privileges of a few individuals'; but as social and economic conditions in England changed, so the liberties and privileges contained in the Charter were gradually extended to include a much wider section of the population. When the English pressed for the enlargement of their civil liberties, they found the existence of the Charter of immense value: 'it gave weight and authority to their measures; afforded a clue to direct them in the mazes of political speculation; and encouraged them to proceed with boldness in completing a plan, the utility of which had already been put to the test of experience'.[2]

Unlike the majority of his contemporaries, Millar studied the actual provisions of the Charter.[3] He attempted to analyse the motivation behind the barons' action against John, in particular he tried to find out exactly what they meant when they demanded 'the restoration of the laws of Edward the Confessor'. After disproving the existence of a body of Saxon statutes, he concluded that the real aim of the barons was 'the recovery of the allodial property, and the independence which they had formerly enjoyed'.[4] Millar's assessment of the Charter contains two other perceptive comments. First, he showed that from the

[1] For a detailed study of this movement see D. Forbes, 'Historismus in England', 4 *Cambridge Journal* (1951), 387–400.

[2] *An Historical View of the English Government* (1787), 298 and 299.

[3] Millar was helped in his task by the existence of Blackstone's edition of the Charter, see above, p. 58 n. 3.

[4] *Historical View*, 271.

Norman Conquest to the reign of Edward I, royal power was steadily increasing. He substantiated this claim by taking the Charters of Henry I, John, and Henry III and comparing the clauses relating to scutage and wardship. His conclusion was that 'the nobility were daily becoming more moderate in their claims', and they had to accept a considerable extension of the prerogative and content themselves with preventing 'wanton abuse' of royal power. Magna Carta, far from reducing the prerogative, was a containing measure 'to prevent [royal] authority from encroaching so rapidly as it might otherwise have done'.[1] The second point made by Millar concerns the clauses relating to trade and commerce, which he saw as evidence of the emergence of the merchant class. But he was quick to point out that the shortness and vagueness of these clauses indicated that this class had not achieved great influence as yet.[2] Thus, by the application of critical and analytical techniques to the study of the past, Millar rejected many of the pseudo-historical beliefs of his contemporaries and restored the Charter to its thirteenth-century feudal context.

Edmund Burke, in his *Abridgment of English History*,[3] similarly stressed the feudal nature of the Charter, which he saw as an attempt to correct abuses which were post-Conquest in origin. He pointed to the limited idea of freedom enunciated in the Charter by the thirteenth-century barons who claimed their liberties, like their lands, from the crown. He rejected the Cokean belief that the Charter was a restoration of Saxon liberties, declaring, 'the constitutions of Magna Charta . . . bear no resemblance, in any particular, to the laws of St. Edward, or

[1] Ibid. 296.
[2] Ibid. 287.
[3] Written in 1757 and published posthumously in 1828. Burke's position *vis-à-vis* the Historical School has been a source of considerable controversy. John Pocock denies Burke a place in the School and interprets his preoccupation with history and historical development as indicative of his close association with the common law tradition of Coke (J. G. A. Pocock, *The Ancient Constitution*, 242 ff., and 'Burke and the Ancient Constitution', 3 *Historical Journal* (1960), 125–43). For the more traditional view see C. E. Merriam, *History of the Theory of Sovereignty since Rousseau* (New York, 1900), and A. Cobban, *Edmund Burke and the Revolt against the Eighteenth Century* (1929).

to any other collection of these ancient institutions'.[1] In his fragmentary *Essay towards an History of the Laws of England*,[2] Burke went further and denied the existence of ancient unalterable law. He described English law as a heterogeneous mixture, a product of change and development: 'in some respects our own; in more borrowed from the policy of foreign nations, and compounded, altered and variously modified, according to the various necessities, which the manners, the religion, and the commerce of the people, have at different times imposed'. He was scornful of those who believed in the perfection of Saxon laws and institutions, who 'would persuade us that the crude institutions of an unlettered people had reached a perfection, which the united efforts of inquiry, experience, learning, and necessity, have not been able to attain in many ages'. He regarded ancient statutes such as the Charter as 'monuments of our pristine rudeness'.[3]

Yet Burke showed a greater appreciation of the Charter, or at least of its political usefulness, in his speeches in the House of Commons;[4] and after the outbreak of revolution in France, he moved closer to the pseudo-historical views of the constitution and the past which he had earlier dismissed. In his *Reflexions*[5] he argued that the English Revolution of 1688, unlike the French Revolution, had been an act of necessity forced upon the people of England in order to preserve the heritage of the past, and repeating the view of Coke and Blackstone that the Charter was a restoration of the 'ancient standing law of the kingdom', he commented 'in the matter of fact, for the greater part, these authors appear to be in the right'.[6] Two years later, writing on the subject of the catholics in Ireland,[7] he went further and declared his belief in the existence of funda-

---

[1] *Works*, x. 535.
[2] Published with the *Abridgment of English History*.
[3] *Works*, x. 555.
[4] See above, p. 55; also *P.H.* 17, 50; *P.H.* 18, 478 ff.; *P.H.* 23 (1782–3), 1312 ff.; *P.H.* 25 (1785–6), 1275; and *P.H.* 29 (1791–2), 646–7.
[5] *Reflexions on the Revolution in France*, written in 1790.
[6] *Works*, v. 76.
[7] *Letter to Sir Hercules Langrishe*, written in 1792.

mental law, asserting that the acts establishing the Church of England were 'a fundamental part of the constitution' in the same way that clause 29 of the Great Charter was fundamental. While not going so far as to deny the validity of statutes made against the principles of the Charter, he now argued that Magna Carta 'is a very venerable law, made by very wise and learned men, and that the legislature, in their attempt to perpetuate it, even against the authority of future parliaments, have shown their judgment that it is *fundamental*'.[1]

Thus, whilst denying the complete and unbroken continuity of English law and institutions, Burke accepted, indeed insisted upon, a large measure of continuity in opposition to Paine's claim that every generation had the right to act as it felt fit. He admired and approved the English custom of claiming rights and privileges 'as a patrimony derived from their forefathers'.[2] Burke, in fact, recognized the heritage of the past, but he was also conscious of the necessity for change in response to circumstances. He regarded the English constitution at once as the product of repeated change and also as embodying a profound character of conscious persistence and conservatism, or, as he expressed it, a 'powerful prepossession towards antiquity' which holds together the English nation.[3] In his view, the English tradition of reverence for antiquity, which he himself shared, drew its justification not from the reputed fact that the constitution had never required or undergone change, but rather from the very different fact that the English people had always tried to preserve, through all their changes, a certain continuity of spirit and character, an organic connection between old and new. He could feel, without real contradiction, that the common law concept of an 'immemorial' public order embodied a real truth, and also that the common law interpretation of English constitutional history was in many respects untenable. Thus the same man who refuted, historically, the

---

[1] *Works*, vi. 328–9.
[2] *Reflexions, Works*, v. 76.
[3] Ibid. See also R. Kirk, 'Burke and the philosophy of prescription', 14 *Journal of the History of Ideas* (1953), 365–80.

claims that Magna Carta had only reiterated the liberties of Saxon times or was itself an adequate expression of the English constitution, could also, without contradiction, approvingly declare that:

from Magna Charta to the Declaration of Rights it has been the uniform policy of our constitution to claim and assert our liberties as an *entailed inheritance* derived to us from our forefathers, and to be transmitted to our posterity . . . By this means our constitution preserves a unity in so great a diversity of its parts.[1]

But more significant perhaps than this transformation of the 'myth' as a consequence of improved understanding of its historical context, the later eighteenth century also saw the development of a new political philosophy which provided a theoretical justification for the fact of parliamentary sovereignty. We discussed in Chapter 3 the gradual extension of parliamentary authority which took place during the course of the eighteenth century. We saw how the English were slow to break completely with the old belief in fundamental law. They still paid lip-service to the customs, traditions, and liberties of the past while at the same time acting in a manner which showed how little limitation such ideas had in practice. They still assumed the conformity of parliament to the ancient principles of law while accepting in practice the legal omnicompetence of parliament. This dichotomy is clearly evident in the writings of Blackstone and had a limiting effect upon his view of sovereignty. A comprehensive justification of parliamentary sovereignty was only worked out when Jeremy Bentham and John Austin substituted the principle of utility for the older philosophical theories based on either historical or abstract natural rights, or both.

Bentham's vigorous assertion of the legislative sovereignty of parliament was a direct result of his preoccupation with law reform. English law was certainly cumbrous, intricate, and complex, and Bentham was not alone in stressing the need for

[1] *Reflexions, Works,* v. 77–8.

reform. Blackstone had attempted to remedy some of the defects by providing a clear and accurate commentary, but this was insufficient for the needs of a rapidly changing society. Bentham went much further and attacked both the structure and the content of the English legal system. He believed the chaotic state of English law to be the result of its gradual development by applying precedents from previous decisions to new situations with the help of reference to a vague body of customary law. This practice gave a monopoly of the law to judges and lawyers who had arbitrary power to define what was right and wrong, with no control over their actions other than an unwritten tradition. As he noted, wherever there is unwritten law 'lawyers will be its defenders', for it is the source of their power.[1] It was his determination to end this judicial tyranny which led him to assert the supremacy of statute and the freedom of parliament to legislate without restriction as fresh circumstances demanded.

In his *Book of Fallacies* he exposed the legal fictions and pseudo-historical beliefs which earlier writers, including Blackstone, revered and expounded as part of the fundamental law. He attacked the so-called 'matchless constitution' of England, and asked: 'Why is it that under pain of being *ipso facto* anarchist convict, we must never presume to look at it otherwise than with shut eyes? Because it was the work of our ancestors . . . few of whom could so much as read, and these few had nothing before them that was worth reading.'[2] He had no respect for the past and dismissed its so-called 'wisdom' as the foolishness of the 'cradle of the race'. He declared that 'it is from the folly, not from the wisdom of our ancestors that we have much to learn'.[3] In his own copy of the *Fragment on Government*, Bentham added the comment that this work was 'the very first publication by which men at large are invited to break loose from the trammels of authority and ancestor wisdom in the field of law'.[4]

[1] *A General View of a Complete Code of Laws, Works,* ed. J. Bowring (New York, 1962), iii. 206.
[2] *Works,* ii. 442.   [3] Ibid. 399 and 401.
[4] Ibid. i. 260 n.

Bentham analysed a number of the supposed ancient liberties of the English, including the Great Charter, in order to assess their validity and reality in his own day. While he regretted that new laws were daily made 'in the teeth of Magna Charta',[1] he condemned the old legal view that statutes contrary to the Charter are invalid: 'God forbid, that by all the lawyers in the world, or for any purpose of any argument, I should ever suffer myself to be betrayed into such extravagance; in a subject it would be sedition, in a judge, it would be usurpation, in anybody it would be nonsense.'[2] Bentham not only denied the present validity of the Charter but he also attacked its inherent qualities. Speaking of the need in all legal systems for 'a general law of liberty' to restrain the actions of the government, he admitted that this had been the intention of Magna Carta. However, it had not had this effect because of 'that unfortunate indeterminate expression, "Lex terrae"', which he denounced as 'an imaginary law, which spreads uncertainty over the whole'.[3] Having dismissed the Charter and established that the whole legal system was corrupt, chaotic, and archaic, Bentham demanded a simple codification of the law, a code which

would speak a language familiar to everybody: each one might consult it at his need. It would be distinguished from all other books by its greater simplicity and clearness. The father of a family, without assistance, might take it in his hand and teach it to his children, and give to the precepts of private morality the force and dignity of public morals.[4]

This, in fact, was just how many Englishmen regarded Magna Carta. Both Beardmore and Burdett expounded the Charter to their children at carefully chosen moments.[5]

Yet despite his rejection of fundamental law, his scorn for

---

[1] *Truth versus Ashhurst, Works*, v. 233.

[2] *Protest against Law-Taxes, Works*, ii. 580.

[3] *Fragment on Government, Works*, i. 576. For the thirteenth-century confusion over 'lex terrae' see J. C. Holt, *Magna Carta*, 266 ff., and F. M. Powicke, 'Per judicium parium vel legem terrae' in *Magna Carta Commemorative Essays*, 96–121.

[4] *A General View of a Complete Code of Laws, Works*, iii. 209.

[5] See above, pp. 60 n. 3 and 69.

history and the achievements of the past, and his claim that the test of utility was the only criterion for assessing institutions, government, and law, Bentham never entirely succeeded in freeing himself from the traditions of Magna Carta. His collateral ends of legislation are, in fact, the same as clause 29; according to Bentham justice must be executed with as little expense, as few delays and vexations as possible.[1] In addition, his attacks on specific abuses of his age were rarely based on the principle of utility, but more often on the principles embodied in clause 29 of the Charter. He deplored the fact that this clause was 'habitually trodden underfoot, without remorse or reclamation' and based his vehement condemnation of the expense of judicial procedure upon it.[2] He also condemned the detention of expired convicts in the colonies as a 'breach of Magna Charta', and declared that the principles of the Charter applied in the colonies as well as in England: 'that over English subjects in England, or anywhere else, the king should by himself or by others, exercise legislative power, without the concurrence of parliament, was repugnant to Magna Charta'. If royal prerogative is admitted in the colonies, Bentham maintained that it must be admitted in England also, and once this happened then 'Magna Charta is waste paper'.[3] Again, protesting against the suggestion for a new and experimental judicatory, Bentham declared that it would contravene the Charter which had always been regarded as 'the stock, root, or foundation of all those liberties whereby the condition of the subjects of this realm stands distinguished to its advantage from that of the subjects of other monarchies'.[4] In his *Securities against Misrule*, Bentham even adopted the language of Coke and Blackstone and claimed 'it is to [the Great Charter and the Bill of Rights] that the English are indebted for every security against misrule'.[5]

Like many of the earlier critics of English law and institutions,

---

[1] *An Introductory View of the Rationale of Evidence, Works*, vi. 10–11.
[2] *Protest against Law-Taxes, Works*, ii. 580.
[3] *A Plea for the Constitution, Works*, iv, 249, 259, and 269.
[4] *Equity Dispatch Court Bill, Works*, iii, 328.   [5] *Works*, viii. 593.

Bentham found a concrete historical precedent such as the Charter of far more weight and significance in attacking specific abuses than abstract philosophical principles. There is, in fact, a considerable degree of inconsistency between Bentham's general principles and theories and his particular criticisms of existing abuses. Although a firm upholder of the complete legislative sovereignty of parliament, he did not discard the principles of Magna Carta, although he never regarded the Charter as exerting any limitation, legal or moral, upon the exercise of that sovereignty.

It was not until the time of John Austin that a serious attempt was made to penetrate in any depth the real basis of sovereign power and to provide a comprehensive theory of legislative sovereignty. Austin empirically examined the laws and institutions of early nineteenth-century England, and stressed the necessity for a clearly known and recognizable sovereign authority in every state. He based his theory of politics upon positive, observable phenomena only and thus rejected any concept of fundamental law derived from history or tradition just as much as the similar concepts deriving from abstract speculative principles. Like Blackstone and Bentham, his theory of sovereignty was determined by his conception of the law. He stressed the sanctions rather than the sources of law which he defined in Hobbesian terms as 'a creature of the actual sovereign', binding because of the sanctions which the sovereign is able to attach to it.[1] Like Bentham, he was concerned to distinguish between law and myth, but, unlike Bentham, he was consistent and thorough in his rejection of such 'unmeaning abstractions' and 'senseless fictions' as fundamental or natural law. He condemned those who are 'led by their ears and not by the principle of utility', and commented with derision 'a sacred or unalienable right is truly and indeed *invaluable*: For, seeing that it means nothing, there is nothing with which it can be measured'.[2]

---

[1] *Lectures on Jurisprudence* (4th edn., 1879), i. 337.
[2] Ibid. 122 and 123.

Liberty, to Austin as to Hobbes, is dependent upon the sovereign; it is merely 'the liberty from legal obligation, which is left or granted by a sovereign government to any of its own subjects'; it originates from the sovereign and can be removed at any time at the sovereign's 'pleasure and discretion'. Austin regarded the quantification of liberties as a very uncertain, often erroneous criterion of judgement for good government, for 'it may consist of freedom from restraints which are required by the common weal, and which the government would lay upon its subjects, if it fulfilled its duties'.[1] Utility, not liberty, is the only true criterion for good government to Austin, who declared, 'the proper purpose or end of a sovereign political government, or the purpose or end for which it ought to exist, is the greatest possible advancement of human happiness'.[2] He drew a sharp line between law proper and custom, declaring the latter to be merely the product of judicial decision:

in spite . . . of the grandiloquous talk by which it has been extolled and obscured, customary law has nothing of the magnificent or mysterious about it . . . it is formed or fashioned by the judges . . . upon pre-existing rules observed spontaneously or wholly deriv-ing their imperfect obligatory force from the religious or moral sanctions.[3]

Custom is therefore a cause and not a source of law; it only becomes law when endorsed and enforced by the sovereign, and cannot limit the sovereign as 'supreme power limited by positive law is a flat contradiction in words'.[4]

Yet Austin did recognize two limitations upon sovereignty: first, divine law, which decrees that government must be in accordance with the test of utility;[5] and second, he admitted a moral limitation, what he called 'rules set and enforced by *mere opinion*, that is, by the opinions or sentiments held or felt by an indeterminate body of men in regard to human conduct'.[6] These are not legal limitations, but rather, as Austin

---

[1] Ibid. 281 and 284.   [2] Ibid. 298.
[3] Ibid. ii. 560.   [4] Ibid. i. 270.
[5] Ibid. 284. See also ibid. 281.   [6] Ibid. 88.

himself said, 'ethical maxims which the sovereign spontaneously observes'.[1] Austin's theory thus allows for the influence
of the Charter as a statement of legal principles which are
generally accepted by the nation and to which the sovereign
authority is expected to adhere. But he rejected the whole
tradition of Magna Carta as the embodiment of fundamental
immemorial law. In its place, he erected an empirical, unlimited,
and omnicompetent sovereign which is the source of all law
and authority. By 1832, with the publication of Austin's
Lectures on Jurisprudence, customary law as a legal limitation
upon sovereignty may, indeed, be regarded as 'belonging to a
past order of things'.[2]

[1] *Lectures on Jurisprudence*, ii. 771.
[2] W. J. Brown, *The Austinian Theory of Law* (1906), 161.

7

The Charter Repealed

The wisdom of ages has made [Magna Carta] venerable, and
stamped it with an authority equal to the *Constitution* itself,
of which it is, in reality, a most essential and *fundamental* part;
so that any attempt to repeal it would be treason to the State!
This glorious Charter must, therefore, ever continue un-
repealed: and even the articles which seem at present useless,
must ever remain in force.[1]

DESPITE this authoritative statement by Granville Sharp, only
four of the original thirty-seven clauses of Henry III's Charter
remain on the statute-book today.[2] The other thirty-three
clauses were repealed between 1828 and 1969, not, as Sharp
predicted, as the result of 'gross depravity and corruption'
indicative of 'total national reprobacy',[3] but as part of a general
movement to reduce, simplify, and clarify the law of England.

Criticism of the state of the law can be found as early as the
sixteenth century when attempts were made to bring about
measures of reform, especially in the field of penal law.[4] But
little was achieved, and by the end of the century dissatisfaction
was widespread. In 1596 Francis Bacon informed Elizabeth I
that laws had 'multiplied in number and slackened in vigour
and execution' during her reign,[5] and indeed Elizabeth and her

---

[1] G. Sharp, *A Declaration of the People's Natural Right to a Share in the Legislature*
(1774), 202–3.

[2] Clauses 1, 9, 29, and 37 (in part). The full text of the Charter is given in the
Appendix, see below, pp. 108–21.

[3] Op. cit. 204.

[4] Proposals were discussed in 1547, 1549, and 1555, while in 1566 a Commission for the executing of penal laws was revoked on grounds that its members
were 'unfit persons' (*C.J.* i. 81).

[5] *Elements of the Common Law of England, Works,* ed. Spedding, Ellis, and Heath
(1857–74), vii. 315.

ministers were fully aware of the need for action. In 1597 Lord Keeper Egerton instructed parliament to review the law and 'where you find superfluity, to prune and cut off; where defect, to supply; and where ambiguity, to explain'.[1] But nothing came of this.

During the following reign both James and his parliaments expressed their support for law reform,[2] and Francis Bacon, who was one of the most consistent and influential advocates of reform, drew up a number of proposals for the amendment and codification of both common and statute law.[3] But although a Select Committee was appointed in 1621 with instructions 'to survey all the statutes, and to draw all the statutes concerning one matter into one plain and perfect law; and to consider which are fit to be continued',[4] no positive revision resulted. While Bacon was pressing for radical reform, Sir Edward Coke attempted to remove some of the uncertainty from English law by providing a clear and orderly commentary in his *Reports* and *Institutes*. But invaluable though this was,[5] the need for through-going reform remained, and by the 1640s there existed a 'general and inbred hatred against both our laws and lawyers'.[6]

The literature of the Interregnum illustrates the extent of the dissatisfaction with the law which existed amongst all sections of the population. The army officers continually pressed parliament to carry out law reform,[7] the City of London petitioned

[1] *P.H.* 1 (1066–1625), 894.

[2] *Political Works of James I*, ed. C. H. McIlwain (Cambridge, Mass., 1918), 292–3 and 311–12; law reform was mentioned in the Great Contract of 1610 (*L.J.* ii. 661).

[3] *Memorial touching the review of penal laws and the amendment of the Common Law* (1614?) *Letters and Life*, ed. Spedding (1861–72), v. 84 ff., and *A Proposition . . . touching the compiling and amendment of the laws* (1614), ibid. vi. 61 ff.

[4] *C.J.* i. 519. Sir Edward Coke was a member of this committee.

[5] Bacon recognized the value of Coke's work, see *A Proposition . . .*, *Letters and Life*, vi. 65.

[6] J. Hare, *England's proper and onely way to an establishment in honour, freedom, peace and happiness* (1648), 6.

[7] See *The Officers' Agreement* (1649), Wolfe, *Leveller Manifestoes*, 353. In 1654 they urged Cromwell to reform the law (*Clarke Papers*, iii. 10–11); even in 1659 they remembered law reform and made it one of their conditions for the restoration of the Rump (*Memoirs of Edmund Ludlow*, ed. C. H. Firth (Oxford, 1894), ii. 75).

parliament for the same ends,[1] and the radicals pursued a vociferous campaign against lawyers and legal abuses. The Levellers were keenly interested in improving the law, but for the most part they attacked not the law itself but the legal system, blaming abuses and inadequacies upon 'Hackney, mercenary Lawyers' and their excessive fees and complex procedure.[2] They frequently contrasted the abuses of their own day with the 'true' principles of law expressed in clause 29 of the Charter.[3] Some of the radicals went further and attacked English law in its entirety. Richard Overton declared that 'the Lawes of this Nation are unworthy a *Free-People*, and deserve from first to last, to be considered, and seriously debated, and reduced to an agreement with common *equity*, and *right reason*, which ought to be the Forme and Life of every Government'.[4] Similar criticism can be found in the writings of Gerrard Winstanley, Samuel Chidley, William Cole, and that 'man of substance', Henry Robinson, who called upon parliament to reform the whole system of law, which he condemned as

a hotch-potch of linsey-wolsey lawes, so numerous, as not to be learned or comprehended, some so differing so that they contradict and give the lye to one another, so irrational and absurd, to spare worse words, so that they character us to be one of the most barbarous people in the world.[5]

Parliament did little to satisfy these demands for law reform.

---

[1] See *The Humble Petition of the Lord Mayor, Aldermen and Commons of the City of London* in *Severall Proceedings in Parliament*, 30 November to 7 December 1649; also *The Representative of Divers well-affected persons in and about the City of London* (1649).
[2] J. Lilburne, *The Peoples Prerogative*, 5. Also see above, p. 17.
[3] See, for example, *The Earnest Petition of many freeborn people* (1648), Haller and Davies, *Leveller Tracts*, 109–10.
[4] *A Remonstrance of many thousand citizens* (1646), Wolfe, op. cit. 124.
[5] *Certaine proposals in order to a new modelling of the lawes* (1653), 3. See also W. K. Jordan, *Men of Substance* (New York, 1942), 191 ff. For Winstanley, see above, p. 23; S. Chidley, *A Cry against a Crying Sin* (1652), *Harl. Misc.* viii. 477–89; W. Cole, *A Rod for the lawyers* (1659), ibid. iv. 319–26; see also J. Ware, *The Corruption and Deficiency of the Laws of England*, ibid. iii. 177–245. On the general question of law reform in the mid seventeenth century see G. B. Nourse, 'Law Reform under the Commonwealth and Protectorate', 75 *L.Q.R.* (1959), 512–29, and D. Veal, *The Popular Movement for Law Reform, 1640–1660* (Oxford, 1970).

In 1650 a parliamentary committee was appointed to review the state of the law, but its only practical achievement was the substitution of English in place of French and Latin as the official language of the courts.[1] After increasing agitation for action, an extra-parliamentary committee was established in 1652 to look into 'inconveniences' in the law.[2] Matthew Hale was one of its leading members, and the proposals which emanated from this lawyer-dominated committee, while they did not satisfy the extreme radicals, would have produced a major reorganization of the English legal system.[3] However, the Rump was preoccupied with more pressing matters than law reform, and nothing was done to put these proposals on the statute-book. The Nominated Parliament, which succeeded the Rump, established its own parliamentary committee to look into the question of law reform and 'consider of a new Body of the law'.[4] This committee, which contained no lawyers, made a number of radical proposals, including the abolition of the Court of Chancery, which aroused the fears of the lawyers and also of moderates such as Cromwell who denounced their proposals as tending to the 'subversion of the Laws and of all the Liberties of this nation'.[5] During the Protectorate, although Cromwell paid lip-service to the need for improving the law,[6] and instructed William Shepard to draw up plans for reform,[7] in practice he failed to press for law reform in the face of increasing conservatism in parliament and amongst the lawyers. Thus, although the Interregnum saw a variety of suggestions for law reform, few of them were implemented,

[1] *C.J.* vi. 487 and 500. Even this reform did not survive the Restoration.
[2] *C.J.* vii. 74.
[3] For details of their proposals see *Several draughts of acts, Somers*, vi. 177–245. For an assessment of the work of this committee see M. Cotterell, 'Interregnum Law Reform, the Hale Commission of 1652', 83 *E.H.R.* (1968), 689–704.
[4] *C.J.* vii. 304. For a discussion of the work of this parliament see *An Exact Relation of the Proceedings and Transactions of the late Parliament* . . . (1654), *Somers*, vi. 266–84. This tract is probably the work of 'Praise God' Barebone.
[5] T. Carlyle, *The Letters and Speeches of Oliver Cromwell*, ed. S. C. Lomas (1904), iii. 99.
[6] Ibid. ii. 541.
[7] *Clarke Papers*, iii. 61, 64, and 76.

partly owing to the political instability of the time which
made constitutional reform the major preoccupation partly
because of disagreement among those pressing for reform,
and partly because of the hostility of the lawyers who,
although they recognized the need to correct abuses, were
determined to maintain the ancient law in the face of radical
attack from naïve and impractical laymen.

After these years of vociferous agitation for law reform, the
subject was dropped after the Restoration and remained forgot-
ten for more than a century.[1] The explanation for this is to be
found initially in the widespread fear of change of any kind
which was a reaction against the experiments of the Interregnum, and then in the complacency and satisfaction with law
and the constitution following the Glorious Revolution. However, criticism began to re-emerge during the course of the
eighteenth century. The social and economic developments of
the century necessitated a mass of regulations which added a
new burden to the already vast and chaotic body of law. In
this situation Blackstone attempted to follow the example of
Coke and provide a clarification and summary of the law,
whereas Bentham, like Bacon before him, had a more ambitious
remedy.[2] Although Bentham's proposals for codification were
too radical to receive support, the necessity for some measure
of reform was slowly becoming recognized. In 1796 a committee appointed by the Commons to investigate 'temporary
expiring laws' complained that:

Statute Law has through a Series of Six Centuries, accumulated at
length to a most voluminous Mass, which is rapidly increasing, and
has been more than doubled in Bulk within the last Fifty Years . . .
[It is] in many Places discordant; in many Places obsolete; in others
perplexed by its miscellaneous Composition of Incongruities; and
that its Style is for the most Part verbose, tautologous, and obscure.

They produced a list of some 1,000 obsolete laws going
back to the reign of Edward III, and recommended the drawing

[1] A committee was appointed in October 1666 to consider law reform, but
nothing came of its work (*C.J.* viii. 631).   [2] See above, pp. 83–4.

up of a 'complete and authoritative publication of the statutes' as a necessary preliminary step to reform.[1] This was achieved between 1810 and 1822, when nine folio volumes of statutes were published containing enactments up to 1713. These were to form the starting-point for the statute law revision movement, but before that got under way, Magna Carta attracted the attention of those attempting to consolidate the law.

In 1816 a motion calling for consolidation was proposed in the Lords by Earl Stanhope, who described the statute-book as 'a perfect hotch-pot—a chaos of darkness, disorder and confusion'. He drew attention to the sheer volume of the statutes and also to what he called the 'vile phraseology' of modern statutes which he contrasted with the 'clear, brief and intelligible' language of the Great Charter.[2] After some discussion on practicability and expense, parliament agreed to appoint a legal expert to draw up a digest of the law along the lines suggested by Stanhope.[3] Little was achieved, however, apart from a number of consolidating acts in the twenties relating to customs and excise, the slave trade, and criminal law. It was the consolidation of criminal law which brought the Charter within the scope of repeal for the first time.

Agitation against the severity of the criminal law, which had preoccupied Englishmen in the sixteenth and seventeenth centuries, was organized in the early nineteenth century by Sir Samuel Romilly and Sir James Mackintosh. In 1822 Mackintosh introduced a motion in the Commons calling for a 'scale of punishments adapted to the degree and measure of criminality', and he claimed to find a precedent for his proposal in the Great Charter: 'remarkable it was that those whom we, in this enlightened age, were apt to consider as barbarians, had legislated respecting crimes with the clearest judgement, and

---

[1] *C.J.* li. 702 ff.
[2] *P.D.* 34 (1816), 173–83. He also contrasted them with 'the language of the unwritten law'! His father, the second earl, had presented a copy of the Articles of the Barons to the British Museum in 1769 (A. N. Newman, *The Stanhopes of Chevening* (1969), 118).   [3] *P.D.* 34, 425 and 1041–3.

with the most careful humanity'.[1] But it was not until the support of Sir Robert Peel was secured that the criminal law was reformed. Between 1826 and 1832 a series of statutes were passed under Peel's direction which consolidated criminal law and reduced the number of crimes punishable by death. One of these, the Offences against the Person Act of 1828, repealed over fifty 'obsolete and intricate' enactments, including clause 26 of the Charter which concerned criminal writs.[2]

By the middle of the nineteenth century the necessity for law reform was recognized and accepted by both political parties and by the majority of lawyers. As Macaulay stated in 1852: 'No observant man can fail to perceive that there is in the public mind a general, a growing, an earnest, and at the same time, I must say, a most sober and remarkable desire for extensive law reform.'[3] From this time onwards the law was in a state of continuous revision and amendment. But although there was general agreement on the need for reform, there was considerable disagreement over the best procedure to adopt for achieving reform. Some lawyers, notably Benenden Ker, were in favour of beginning with consolidation; others, such as Chisholme Anstey, insisted on the necessity of removing obsolete enactments from the statute-book before embarking on the task of consolidation.[4] Up to 1860 Ker's policy of immediate consolidation had greater support and, indeed, some success was achieved.[5] But this was a difficult, complex, and expensive method and it was abandoned in the sixties for the more limited procedure suggested by Anstey. It was the application of this criterion of obsolescence which resulted in the first major reduction of Magna Carta.

In 1860 two legal experts were appointed to review the statute-book and list all obsolete enactments. The results of

[1] *P.D.*, new series, 7 (1822), 793. See also *P.D.*, new series, 9 (1823), 405.
[2] 9 George IV, c. 31, s. I.
[3] *Selected Speeches*, ed. G. M. Young (1935), 326–7.
[4] See P.P. 1854 (301), 24, for Anstey's views and P.P. 1854 (302), 24, for Ker's.
[5] For example, seven Criminal Law Consolidation Acts were passed in 1861 (24 & 25 Victoria, cc. 94–100). These were based on the reports of the Royal Commissions of 1833 and 1849.

their work can be seen in the Statute Law Revision Acts of 1861 and 1863;[1] the first repealed some 900 enactments since 1770, while the second dealt with earlier statutes and included large portions of the Charter. Presenting the 1863 Bill, the Lord Chancellor, Lord Westbury, stated that the enactments chosen for repeal were 'those which are no longer applicable to the modern state of society—enactments which have become wholly obsolete'. But he explained that certain ancient statutes 'connected with our political rights and institutions' had been left outside the scope of revision, and he assured the Lords that these statutes, which he called 'stones in the edifice of the constitution', would remain intact: 'no enactment or statute is touched that may be considered to have entered into the common law, or formed the foundation of any rule of practice or procedure, or may be referred to as the basis on which the right or title of property is made to rest'.[2] Yet this Bill included seventeen clauses of the Great Charter, a statute which the opinion of centuries had firmly established as a venerable 'edifice of the constitution' and worthy of complete preservation on Westbury's professed criterion. This inconsistency went unnoticed in the Lords, where the Bill passed without comment; but its reception in the Commons was more critical. Mr. Pope Hennessy strongly objected to the idea of repealing parts of the Charter, and he proposed an amendment excluding the Charter and other 'landmarks of the constitution'.[3] He was unsuccessful, however, and Magna Carta was reduced by almost half. The clauses of the Charter which were repealed by this Revision Act related to feudal incidents; clauses 5 (in part), 24, 27, 31, 33, 36, and 37 (in part) were included on the grounds of their obsolescence, and clauses 2–6, 13, 19–21, 28, and 34 because of their virtual repeal by previous enactments.[4] This was a reasonable and justifiable

---

[1] 24 & 25 Victoria, c. 101, and 26 & 27 Victoria, c. 125.
[2] *P.D.*, 3rd series, 171 (1863), 775 ff.
[3] Ibid., 172 (1863), 1227.
[4] Chiefly the Tenures Abolition Act of 1660 by which Charles II gave up his feudal dues in return for a parliamentary grant.

revision on grounds of relevance and clarity. The only inconsistency in the selection of clauses for repeal was the omission of clause 10, dealing with distress for service. But the phrase 'nor any freehold' may have suggested wider implications relating to property, thus preventing the repeal of this clause as a purely feudal regulation.

These revision acts made possible the publication of a revised edition of statutes which was completed in 1885. But the eighteen volumes of this edition were still considered too many, and a new phase of revision began, preparatory to the publication of a shorter and cheaper edition.[1] During this process five more clauses of the Charter were removed. In 1879 clauses 11 and 12 were repealed by the Civil Procedure Acts Repeal Act, in 1887 the Sheriffs Act repealed clause 35, and in 1887 and 1892 two general Statute Law Revision Acts removed clauses 32 and 17 respectively.[2] These five clauses, concerning legal procedure and alienation of land, had no relevance by the late nineteenth century and passed through parliament without comment.

The work of revision continued in the twentieth century. In 1925 the Administration of Estates Act replaced clauses 7 and 18 (in part), and the remainder of clause 18 was repealed by the Crown Proceedings Act of 1947.[3] Preparations now began for a third edition of *Statutes Revised*,[4] and the Statute Law Revision Act of 1948 was drawn up to facilitate this. It removed three more clauses of the Charter; clauses 10 and 22 were regarded as obsolete, and clause 25 had been partly superseded and was partly obsolete.[5] Thus, within the space of some 100 years, twenty-eight clauses of Magna Carta were removed from the statute-book.[6]

---

[1] Twenty-four volumes of this second edition were published between 1888 and 1929.
[2] 42 & 43 Victoria, c. 59, 50 & 51 Victoria, c. 55, 50 & 51 Victoria, c. 59, and 55 & 56 Victoria, c. 19.
[3] 15 & 16 George V, c. 23, and 10 & 11 George VI, c. 44.
[4] Published in 1950 in thirty-two volumes.
[5] 11 & 12 George VI, c. 62.
[6] Strictly twenty-seven and a half, for clause 7 was repealed with saving.

But the statute law revision movement which brought about this reduction of the Charter was limited by the very nature of its procedure. Statutes were only repealed if it could be shown that they were no longer in force,[1] and great care was taken to avoid enactments on which there might be doubt or disagreement as to their continuing validity. In addition, each of the general statute law revision acts contained an elaborate saving clause,[2] so that, if a mistake was made, the legal principle expressed in the repealed enactment could be applied by the courts—and indeed was applied in a number of cases.[3] As the task of revision was in the hands of a voluntary Statute Law Committee, this too had a limiting effect upon the achievements of the revision movement. But a significant change took place in 1965 with the establishment of the Law Commission. For the first time a permanent, full-time body was set up by parliament, with instruction to:

take and keep under review all the law . . . with a view to its systematic development and reform, including in particular the codification of such law, the elimination of anomalies, the repeal of obsolete and unnecessary enactments, the reduction of the number of separate enactments and generally the simplification and modernisation of the law.[4]

The Commission, which is composed of five lawyers appointed by the Lord Chancellor and financed by an annual grant from parliament, has not only given a new impetus to the process of law reform but has developed a new approach to the question of statute revision.

Following the example of the earlier reformers, the Law Commissioners quickly turned their attention to the question

---

[1] There were six classes of enactment which fitted this criterion: those which were expired, spent, repealed in general terms, virtually repealed, superseded, and obsolete; see P.P. 1927 (211), iii.

[2] First included in the Statute Law Revision Act of 1863 and thereafter included in all general statute law revision acts.

[3] In *Leeds Industrial Co-operative Society Ltd.* v. *Slack* jurisdiction conferred by a statute repealed by the Statute Law Revision Act of 1883 was held to be still in force by virtue of the saving clause; [1924] A.C. 851. See also *Cowper* v. *Laidler*, [1903] 2 Ch. 337.

[4] Law Commissions Act, 1965, c. 22.

of criminal law. In 1966 they produced a Bill to amend the criminal law that included clause 14 of the Charter among obsolete enactments to be repealed. It is perhaps surprising that this clause, which had been revered for centuries as enunciating the principle that sentence must be in accordance with the nature and gravity of the offence, should have been removed with such ease. Even the press remained silent and in parliament only Viscount Colville expressed dismay at its inclusion. After being informed that this clause was concerned only with amercements, 'a wholly obsolete penalty',[1] he withdrew his opposition and the Bill passed without further comment.[2]

The repeal of clause 14 was merely the beginning of the Law Commission's interest in the Charter. Turning to the question of statute law revision, they expressed the need for what they called a 'more forceful approach', and stated their intention of working through the statute-book in order to recommend the repeal not just of those enactments which could be shown to be obsolete, but also those which 'cannot be shown to perform a useful function'.[3] The Law Commissioners were fully conscious of the revolutionary nature of this new approach. As their Chairman, Sir Leslie Scarman, said, 'we have nailed our flag to the mast of a ship which traditionally minded observers find hard to identify'.[4] But they were also aware that by the application of this new criterion many of the doubtful enactments which had survived the traditional methods of statute law revision could be removed.[5]

Their first general measure to reduce the number of statutes was entitled the Statute Law (Repeals) Bill rather than the traditional 'Statute Law Revision Bill' in order to indicate its increased scope. This Bill, which covered over 200 enactments, included eight clauses of the Great Charter on the grounds that

[1] Lord Stonham; P.D., Lords, 5th series, 278 (1966–7), 458.
[2] It received the royal assent on 21 July 1967; Criminal Law Act, 1967, c. 58.
[3] First Programme on Consolidation and Statute Law Revision (1966), Law Com., no. 2.
[4] 'Law Reform—The Experience of the Law Commission', 10 Journal of the Society of Public Teachers of Law (1968), 96.
[5] See Law Commission: First Annual Report, 1965–6, Law Com., no. 4.

they were 'of no practical significance today, being either obsolete or superseded by the modern law on the subject'.[1] Only clauses 9 and 29 were left untouched. In addition, various confirmations of the Charter were included for repeal[2] on the grounds that they merely reaffirmed principles expressed in clause 29 and so had only 'historical interest'.[3]

The Joint Committee of Lords and Commons which scrutinized this Bill expressed grave doubts about these proposals. While they accepted the obsolescence of many clauses of the Charter, they questioned the inclusion of clauses 1 and 37 and the various confirmations of the Charter on the grounds that the repeal of these enactments involved a value judgement as to whether in fact they had any further use.[4] The Law Commission openly admitted this, but argued that these were all confirmatory clauses whose existence was superfluous when clause 29 remained on the statute-book.[5] However, the Joint Committee were still not satisfied. Mr. Ian Percival, one of the Commons representatives, warned of the possible danger that 'in getting rid of duplication, we . . . remove the whole of the substructure', and Lord Upjohn, the Chairman of the Joint Committee, argued that enactments which have no operative force may still be of practical utility.[6] The Joint Committee proceeded to remove clauses 1 and 37 and many of the later confirmations of the Charter from the schedule of the Bill.[7] In all, they made thirty amendments to the Bill, one a major alteration involving the removal of one whole clause.[8] In doing

[1] *Statute Law Revision: First Report*, Law Com., no. 22; Cmnd. 4052 (May 1969), Sch. Pt. i. The clauses were 1, 7 (previously repealed with saving), 8, 15, 16, 23, 30, and 37.

[2] 1297, 1327, 1328, 1331, 1340, 1351, 1354, 1368, 1405, 1416, and 1423.

[3] Law Com., no. 22; Cmnd. 4052, Sch. Pt. i.

[4] *Fourth Report by the Joint Committee of Lords and Commons on Consolidation Bills, being a report upon the Statute Law (Repeals) Bill*, House of Commons Papers, (1968–9), 382.

[5] Ibid. 6 ff. [6] Ibid. 15 and 19.

[7] 1351, 1354, 1368, 1405, 1416, and 1423 were restored.

[8] Clause 4, which would have abolished the common law right to enclose common land. This raised worries in some quarters about the ownership of Runnymede meadow and the land given to the American Government for the Kennedy memorial.

so they clearly rejected the new principle put forward by the Law Commission that it is the responsibility of anyone opposing repeal to show that the enactment in question still retains some element of validity; they insisted that the onus of proof lies with the drafters of revision bills, who must provide irrefutable evidence that the enactments put forward for repeal are indeed useless.[1] The amended Bill received the royal assent in October 1969 and came into force on 1 January 1970.[2]

Thus, four clauses of Magna Carta have survived this latest utilitarian attack. Yet the validity of three of them is somewhat dubious. Clause 37 is a general saving clause which has little practical value; it is a declaration of intent rather than a limitation in any sense on the actions of the government. Clause 1, a general confirmation of the privileges of the English Church, has been of little positive use to the Church in the past and is unlikely to prove more so in the future. It is true that this clause was quoted in the sixteenth century by critics of Henry VIII's ecclesiastical policies,[3] and that in the nineteenth century the Oxford reformers opposed state encroachment on grounds of clause 1;[4] but both were doomed to failure. As Lord Brougham forcefully informed the House of Lords in 1833, to uphold the inalienable rights of the Church was a 'gross and monstrous anomaly' contravening the supremacy of parliament.[5] The rights and privileges of the English Church are, in fact, only

---

[1] See speech in the Commons by Percival, *P.D.*, Commons, 5th series, 788 (1968–9), 531 ff., and especially 537.

[2] Statute Law (Repeals) Act, 1969, c. 52. It repealed clauses 7, 8, 15, 16, 23, and 30.

[3] By Archbishop Warham in 1532 (*Letters and Papers, Foreign and Domestic, of the Reign of Henry VIII*, ed. Brewer *et al.* (1862–1932), v. 542); by More at his trial (W. Roper, *Life of Sir Thomas More* (New York, 1962), 248–9); and by those who took part in the Pilgrimage of Grace (*Letters and Papers*, xi. 478). In addition, Thomas Cromwell showed interest in the words 'libera sit' of clause 1 (R. B. Merriman, *Life and Letters of Thomas Cromwell* (Oxford, 1902), i. 102). I am grateful to Professor G. R. Elton for this last reference.

[4] Pusey wrote 'if the State will not, as Magna Charta pledges it, allow that "the Church should have its liberties inviolate", we must ask that the State will set us free from itself' (H. P. Liddon, *Life of E. B. Pusey* (1893–7), iii. 249).

[5] *P.D.*, 3rd series, 19 (1833), 991.

those which parliament allows, and clause 1 of the Charter is too general and vague in its terminology to be of real value in any dispute with parliament. Clause 9, which confirms the liberties of the City of London and other chartered towns, boroughs, and ports, is another rather meaningless confirmation of ancient liberties. Like clause 1, it does not state the liberties which it purports to confirm, and in any case the privileges of these towns are more clearly defined and safeguarded in their own individual charters. At first sight it is difficult to understand why the Law Commissioners neglected to include this clause for repeal among the other confirmatory clauses. But the explanation probably lies in the fact that clause 9 specifically mentions the 'old liberties and customs' of the City of London, and in recent years parliament has shown itself to be unwilling to alter the privileged position of the City. Following the recommendation of the Herbert Commission,[1] the London Government Act of 1963, which reorganized the structure of local government in the Greater London area, left the City intact.[2] More recently, and after much discussion in parliament and the press, the City was excluded from the major changes in the Justices of the Peace Act of 1968.[3] 'Logic', as the Herbert Commission declared, 'has its limits, and the position of the City of London lies outside them.'[4] Thus clause 9, which confirms the privileges of the City, also lies outside the limits of logic and remains on the statute-book.

But it is not from these clauses that the significance of Magna Carta originates or depends. The long-established reputation

---

[1] *Report of the Royal Commission on Local Government in Greater London* (October 1960), Cmnd. 1164.

[2] For a short comment on this Act, see the note by D. G. T. Williams in 27 *Modern Law Review* (1964), 447–54. I am grateful to Mr. Williams for drawing my attention to this Act and to the Justices of the Peace Act in connection with clause 9. Indeed, the remainder of this chapter owes much to the help and advice of Mr. Williams.

[3] Among other things, the Act abolished *ex officio* J.P.s; but the Lord Mayor and Aldermen of the City were excluded. During the debate in the Lords on this question, Lord Denning quoted clause 9 in support of their special position (*P.D.*, Lords, 5th series, 291 (1968), 916–17).

[4] Cmnd. 1164, p. 237.

of the Charter as the safeguard of English liberties derives from clause 29, which Burke believed to be 'engraven on the hearts of Englishmen'.[1] This clause, which expresses the principle that judgement must be available to all men equally and freely, has come to be regarded as a guarantee of law, liberty, and good government, protecting every individual against arbitrary state interference and providing him with a procedure of appeal in the event of any infringement of his liberties, appeal to the judgement of his peers or the law of the land. Yet although clause 29 is widely regarded as a real limitation upon the actions of the executive, it is no more immune from change by parliament than the rest of the Charter; it 'is not condemned to that immunity from development or improvement which we attribute to the law of the Medes and Persians'.[2] Indeed the provisions of this clause have been revoked by parliament on a number of occasions. The suspensions of habeas corpus during the eighteenth and nineteenth centuries were, in effect, suspensions of clause 29, as were the twentieth-century defence of the realm regulations which gave discretionary powers to the government during time of war and suspended the normal legal processes. On these occasions the legal principles expressed in clause 29 were sacrificed on grounds of national security, for as Lord Scrutton declared in 1918, 'a war could not be carried out according to the principles of Magna Charta'.[3]

But it is not only in time of war that fears for the provisions of clause 29 have been expressed. The rapid expansion and increasing complexity of governmental business which has taken place during the twentieth century has resulted in a remarkable growth in the power of the executive, which has been seen as a new threat to individual liberty.[4] In particular, the practice of delegated legislation has created a situation in which the minister is both interpreter and administrator of the

[1] *P.H.* 29 (1791–2), 646.
[2] *Chester* v. *Bateson* (1920), 1 K.B. 829, *per Darling, J.*, at p. 832.
[3] *Ronnfeldt* v. *Phillips* (1918), 35 T.L.R. 46, at p. 47.
[4] The now classic work drawing attention to the dangers of executive authority is Lord Hewart's *The New Despotism* (1929).

details of legislation agreed only in general terms by parliament. Admittedly the minister is responsible to parliament for his actions; but parliament, whose business has increased also, has less time now to provide an adequate check on the actions of the executive. Thus even greater responsibility rests with the courts for the protection of individual rights.

However, the question of judicial review in relation to ministerial powers has been a source of some disagreement. Following the First World War, strict judicial scrutiny was exercised. In 1920 Mr. Justice Darling upheld the courts' right to review and, if necessary, to abrogate ministerial decisions, insisting that the individual's right to free access to the courts was an 'elemental right' which could not be removed by the executive.[1] A year later the Wiltshire Dairies' refusal to pay a levy imposed by the Ministry of Food was sustained by the courts on the grounds that financial exactions need parliamentary, not just executive, sanction.[2] But during the Second World War discretionary powers were once more upheld in the courts, and ministerial authority was declared to be above judicial review. Giving judgement in the now famous case of *Liversidge* v. *Anderson*, Lord Wright declared, 'I cannot see any ground for holding that the performance of [the Minister's duty to act in the national interest] is to be subject to the decision of a judge.'[3] But Lord Atkin, dissenting from a decision which, he said, gave 'an uncontrolled power of imprisonment to the minister', firmly and clearly insisted on the necessity for judicial

[1] *Chester* v. *Bateson*, at p. 834. This is an interesting case, for Mr. Justice Darling rejected the claimant's argument based on Magna Carta, clause 29 on the ground that a later statute (in this case the Defence of the Realm Act) is superior to an earlier statute; but he then proceeded to uphold the common law principle expressed in clause 29 as an 'elemental right' above executive interference. In other words, he separated the principles of fundamental law from its enactments.

[2] (1921), 37 T.L.R. 884, and (1922), 38 T.L.R. 781. Magna Carta figured large in the Dairies' case, but judgement was given on grounds of the Bill of Rights. In 1939 the Emergency Powers (Defence) Act gave the Treasury authority to impose financial exactions and thus prevented a recurrence of judicial decisions like this one of 1921.

[3] [1942] A.C. 206, at pp. 265–6. In this case, the courts upheld the Home Secretary's discretionary right to detain aliens.

review.[1] After the war, although the general principle of judicial review was reasserted, in practice the courts tended to adopt what David Williams has called 'a self-denying ordinance',[2] and this has led many people to complain that judicial scrutiny of executive action is inadequate.[3] However, there are signs that the courts are now prepared to be more critical of the exercise of discretionary powers.[4]

The courts have also begun to question the extent of the use of crown privilege. This doctrine, which according to David Williams 'epitomises judicial indulgence towards the executive',[5] has been used increasingly since the Thetis case of 1942 in which the courts upheld the minister's right to withhold documentary evidence.[6] But recently the indiscriminate use of crown privilege has been condemned by the courts and some progress has been achieved in limiting this abuse.[7] As Lord Salmon has stressed, the 'residual power' of the courts to refuse crown privilege must be exercised if the courts 'are to preserve their function of protecting the vital interest of the public in seeing that justice is done'.[8] Too often, however, the courts

[1] Ibid., at p. 244.

[2] *Not in the Public Interest* (1965), 187.

[3] Williams, op. cit.; C. J. Hamson, *Executive Discretion and Judicial Control* (1954); J. D. B. Mitchell, 'The Constitutional Implications of Judicial Control', 25 *Cambridge Law Journal* (1967), 46–61; and H. Street, *Justice in the Welfare State* (1968).

[4] For example, *Padfield* v. *Ministry of Agriculture, Fisheries & Food*, [1968] 1 All E.R. 694 in which the Minister's refusal to hold an inquiry was held to be unlawful and a writ of mandamus to compel an inquiry to be held was granted. Professor H. W. R. Wade has described that decision as 'the rejection of the whole idea of unfettered discretion' ('The Myth of Unfettered Discretion', 84 *L.Q.R.* (1968), 168). Even more significantly, in 1969 the House of Lords nullified a decision by the Foreign Compensation Commission despite the fact that the statute establishing this Commission (Foreign Compensation Act, 1950) had specifically stated that its decisions could not be questioned in a court of law (*Anisminic Ltd.* v. *The Foreign Compensation Commission*, [1969] 1 All E.R. 208).

[5] *Not in the Public Interest*, 191 ff.

[6] *Duncan* v. *Cammell, Laird & Co. Ltd.*, [1942] A.C. 624.

[7] For example, *Re Grosvenor Hotel, London (No. 2)*, [1964] 3 All E.R. 354; *Wednesbury Corporation* v. *Ministry of Housing & Local Government*, [1965] 1 W.L.R. 261, and especially *Conway* v. *Rimmer*, [1968] 1 All E.R. 874.

[8] *Re Grosvenor Hotel, London (No. 2)*, at p. 372. See also *The Times* report (4 July 1969) of Lord Salmon's 'indignant address' to a meeting of Justice, entitled 'The Bench as the last bulwark of individual liberty'.

have failed to exercise this power, with the result that there is a widespread feeling that the courts are no longer providing adequate protection for the individual against executive action, and this has led to agitation in parliament and the press for new safeguards for individual rights.

Some success was achieved in 1967 with the appointment of a Parliamentary Commissioner for Administration as a result of which the individual now has an additional parliamentary means of redress against maladministration.[1] The same concern to limit executive action can be seen behind the recent proposals for a new Bill of Rights to provide statutory safeguards for the 'inalienable rights and liberties of the subject'.[2] Such actions, and the widespread support which they have received, are indicative of the continuing strength of the basic principles of law and government expressed in clause 29 of Magna Carta. It may well be true that equitable justice and responsible government are better secured by more recent enactments. It may also be true that these ends are inadequately safeguarded by existing legislation and need to be given modern statutory backing. But as long as these principles are valued and defended, the Charter will always retain its reputation and its power over the national imagination.

For more than seven centuries Magna Carta has inspired as well as protected individual liberties. It began its long career in the hands of the barons of the thirteenth century; it subsequently passed into the keeping of the common law opponents of the prerogative and then became the property of both conservative constitutionalists and radical agitators. It is now part of the heritage of the English people whose responsibility

---

[1] Parliamentary Commissioner Act, 1967, c. 13. Yet this is a very limited measure, 'a half-hearted affair, hinged about with restrictions and exceptions' according to Professor Harry Street, *Justice in the Welfare State*, 116.

[2] Motion proposed by Emlyn Hooson, M.P. for Montgomery, on 22 July 1969 (*P.D.*, Commons, 5th series, 787 (1968–9), 1519). See also Lord Lambton's efforts on the same lines in April 1969 (ibid. 782 (1968–9), 474 ff.) and Lord Wade's motion of June 1969 (*P.D.*, Lords, 5th series, 302 (1969), 1026 ff.). More recently, Lord Shawcross, Chairman of the Council of Justice, reiterated the need for 'a new Magna Carta for the little man' (*The Times*, 25 June 1970).

it is to preserve the Charter not only for what it originally was, but for what it has meant and still means in spirit as well as in letter. As Sir James Mackintosh wrote in 1830:

To have produced [Magna Carta], and to have preserved it, to have matured it, constitute the immortal claim of England on the esteem of mankind. Her Bacons and her Shakespeares, her Miltons and Newtons, with all the truth which they have revealed, and all the generous virtue which they have inspired, are of inferior value when compared with the subjection of men and their rulers to the principles of justice; if, indeed, it be not more true that these mighty spirits could not have been formed except under equal laws, nor roused to full activity without the influence of that spirit which the Great Charter breathed over their forefathers.[1]

[1] *History of England* (1830), i, 221–2.

Appendix

MAGNA CARTA (1297)

THE following text is taken from *Statutes at Large*, ed. O. Ruffhead, revised C. Runnington (1786–1800), i. 1–10.

Edward by the grace of God King of *England*, Lord of *Ireland*, and Duke of *Guyan*, to all *Archbishops, Bishops*, etc. We have seen the Great Charter of the Lord *Henry*, sometimes King of *England*, our father, of the Liberties of *England*, in these words: HENRY by the grace of God, King of *England*, Lord of *Ireland*, Duke of *Normandy* and *Guyan*, and Earl of *Anjou*, to all Archbishops, Bishops, Abbots, Priors, Earls, Barons, Sheriffs, Provosts, Officers, and to all Bailiffs and other our faithful Subjects, which shall see this present Charter, Greeting. Know ye that we, unto the Honour of Almighty God, and for the salvation of the souls of our progenitors and successors, *Kings of England*, to the advancement of holy Church, and amendment of our Realm, of our meer and free will, have given and granted to all Archbishops, Bishops, Abbots, Priors, Earls, Barons, and to all freemen of this our realm, these liberties following, to be kept in our kingdom of *England* for ever.

CAP. I

A Confirmation of Liberties

First, We have granted to God, and by this our present Charter have confirmed, for us and our Heirs for ever, That the Church of *England* shall be free, and shall have her whole rights and liberties inviolable. (2) We have granted also, and given to all the freemen of our realm, for us and our Heirs for ever, these liberties underwritten, to have and to hold to them and their Heirs, of us and our Heirs for ever.

CAP. II

The Relief of the King's Tenant of full Age

If any of our Earls or Barons, or any other, which holdeth of Us in chief by Knights service, die and at the time of his death his heir be of full age, and oweth us Relief, he shall have his inheritance by the old Relief; that is to say, the heir or heirs of an Earl, for a whole Earldom, by one hundred pound; the heir or heirs of a Baron, for an whole Barony, by one hundred marks; the heir or heirs of a Knight, for one whole Knights fee, one hundred shillings at the most; and he that hath less, shall give less, according to the old custom of the fees.

CAP. III

The Wardship of an Heir within Age.
The Heir a Knight

But if the Heir of any such be within age, his Lord shall not have the ward of him, nor of his land, before that he hath taken of him homage. (2) And after that such an heir hath been in ward (when he is come of full age) that is to say, to the age of one and twenty years, he shall have his inheritance without Relief, and without Fine; so that if such an heir, being within age, be made Knight, yet nevertheless his land shall remain in the keeping of his Lord unto the term aforesaid.

CAP. IV

No Waste shall be made by a Guardian
in Wards Lands

The keeper of the land of such an heir, being within age, shall not take of the lands of the heir, but reasonable issues, reasonable customs, and reasonable services, and that without destruction and waste of his men and his goods. (2) And if we commit the custody of any such land to the Sheriff, or to any other, which is answerable unto us for the issues of the same land, and he make destruction or waste of those things that he hath in custody, we will take of him amends *and recompence therefore*, (3) and the land shall be committed to two lawful and discreet men of that fee, which shall answer unto us for the issues of the same land, or unto him whom we will assign. (4) And if we give or sell to any man the custody of any such land, and he therein do make destruction or waste, he shall lose the same custody; and it shall be assigned to two lawful and discreet men of that fee, which also in like manner shall be answerable to us, as afore is said.

CAP. V

Guardians shall maintain the Inheritance of their Wards; and of Bishoprics, etc.

The keeper, so long as he hath the custody of the land of such an heir, shall keep up the houses, parks, warrens, ponds, mills, and other things pertaining to the same land, with the issues of the said land; and he shall deliver to the Heir, when he cometh to his full age, all his land stored with ploughs, and all other things, at the least as he received it. All these things shall be observed in the custodies of Archbishopricks, Bishopricks, Abbeys, Priories, Churchs, and Dignities vacant, which appertain to us; except this, that such custody shall not be sold.

CAP. VI

Heirs shall be married without Disparagement

Heirs shall be married without Disparagement.

CAP. VII

A Widow shall have her Marriage, Inheritance, and Quarentine. The King's Widow, etc.

A Widow, after the death of her husband, incontinent, and without any Difficulty, shall have her marriage and her inheritance,

(2) and shall give nothing for her dower, her marriage, or her inheritance, which her husband and she held the day of the death of her husband, (3) and she shall tarry in the chief house of her husband by forty days after the death of her husband, within which days her dower shall be assigned her (if it were not assigned her before) or that the house be a castle; (4) and if she depart from the castle, then a competent house shall be forthwith provided for her, in the which she may honestly dwell, until her dower be to her assigned, as it is aforesaid; and she shall have in the meantime her reasonable estovers of the common; (5) and for her dower shall be assigned unto her the third part of all the lands of her husband, which were his during coverture, except she were endowed of less at the Church-door. (6) No widow shall be distrained to marry herself: nevertheless she shall find surety, that she shall not marry without our licence and assent (if she hold of us) nor without the assent of the Lord, if she hold of another.

CAP. VIII

How Sureties shall be charged to the King

We or our Bailiffs shall not seize any land or rent for any debt, as long as the present Goods and Chattels of the debtor do suffice to pay the debt, and the debtor himself be ready to satisfy therefore. (2) Neither shall the pledges of the debtor be distrained, as long as the principal debtor is sufficient for the payment of the debt. (3) And if the principal debtor fail in the payment of the debt, having nothing wherewith to pay, or will not pay where he is able, the pledges shall answer for the debt. (4) And if they will, they shall have the lands and rents of the debtor, until they be satisfied of *that* which they before paid for him, except that the debtor can show himself to be acquitted against the said sureties.

CAP. IX

The Liberties of London, *and other Cities and Towns confirmed*

The city of *London* shall have all *the* old liberties and customs, *which it hath been used to have.* Moreover we will and grant, that all other Cities, Boroughs, Towns, and the Barons of the Five Ports, and all other Ports, shall have all their liberties and free customs.

CAP. X

None shall distrain for more Service than is due

No man shall be distrained to do more service for a Knights fee, nor any freehold, than therefore is due.

CAP. XI

Common Pleas shall not follow the King's Court

Common Pleas shall not follow our Court, but shall be holden in some place certain.

CAP. XII

Where and before whom Assises shall be taken. Adjournment for Difficulty

Assises of *novel disseisin,* and of *Mortdancestor,* shall not be taken but in the shires, and after this manner: If we be out of this Realm, our chief Justicer shall send our Justicers through every County once in the Year, which, with the Knights of the shires, shall take the said Assises in those counties; (2) and those things that at the coming of our foresaid Justicers, being sent to take those Assises in the counties, cannot be determined, shall be ended by them in some other place in their circuit; (3) and those things, which for difficulty of some articles cannot be determined by them, shall be referred to our Justicers of the Bench, and there shall be ended.

CAP. XIII

Assises of Darrein Presentment

Assises of *Darrein Presentment* shall be alway taken before our Justices of the Bench, and there shall be determined.

CAP. XIV

How Men of all Sorts shall be amerced, and by whom

A Freeman shall not be amerced for a small fault, but after the manner of the fault; and for a great fault after the greatness thereof, saving to him his contenement; (2) and a Merchant likewise, saving to him his Merchandise; (3) and any other's villain than ours shall be likewise amerced, saving his wainage, if he falls into our mercy. (4) And none of the said amerciaments shall be assessed, but by the oath of honest and lawful men of the vicinage. (5) Earls and Barons shall not be amerced but by their Peers, and after the manner of their offence. (6) No man of the Church shall be amerced after the quantity of his spiritual Benefice, but after his Lay-tenement, and after the quantity of his offence.

CAP. XV

Making of Bridges and Banks

No Town or Freeman shall be distrained to make Bridges nor Banks, but such as of old time and of right have been accustomed to make them in the time of King *Henry* our Grandfather.

CAP. XVI

Defending of Banks

No Banks shall be defended from henceforth, but such as were in defence in the time of King Henry our Grandfather, by the same places, and the same bounds, as they were wont to be in his time.

CAP. XVII

Holding Pleas of the Crown

No Sheriff, Constable, Escheator, Coroner, nor any other our Bailiffs, shall hold Pleas of our Crown.

CAP. XVIII

The King's Debtor dying, the King shall be first paid

If any that holdeth of us Lay-fee do die, and our Sheriff or Bailiff do show our Letters Patents of our summon for Debt, which the dead man did owe to us; it shall be lawful to our Sheriff or Bailiff to attach or inroll all the goods and chattels of the dead, being found in the said fee, to the Value of the same Debt, by the sight *and testimony* of lawful men, so that nothing thereof shall be taken away, until we be clearly paid off the debt; (2) and the residue shall remain to the Executors to perform the testament of the dead; (3) and if nothing be owing unto us, all the chattels shall go to the use of the dead (saving to his wife and children their reasonable parts).

CAP. XIX

Purveyance for a Castle

No Constable, nor his Bailiff, shall take corn or other chattels of any man, if the man be not of the Town where the Castle is, but he shall forthwith pay for the same, unless that the will of the seller was to respite the payment; (2) and if he be of the same Town, the price shall be paid unto him within forty days.

CAP. XX

Doing of Castle-ward

No Constable shall distrain any Knight to give money for keeping of his Castle, if he himself will do it in his proper person, or cause it to be done by another sufficient man, if he may not do it himself for a reasonable cause. (2) And if we lead or send him to an army, he shall be free from Castle-ward for the time that he shall be with us in fee in our host, for the which he hath done service in our wars.

CAP. XXI

Taking of Horses, Carts, and Wood

No Sheriff nor Bailiff of ours, or any other, shall take the Horses or Carts of any man to make carriage, except he pay the old price limited, that is to say, for carriage with two horse, x.d. a day; for three horse, xiv.d. a day. (2) No demesne Cart of any Spiritual person or Knight, or any Lord, shall be taken by our Bailiffs; (3) nor we, nor our Bailiffs, nor any other, shall take any man's wood for our Castles, or other our necessaries to be done, but by the licence of him whose wood it shall be.

CAP. XXII

How long Felons Lands shall be holden by the King

We will not hold the Lands of them that be convict of Felony but one year and one day, and then those Lands shall be delivered to the Lords of the fee.

CAP. XXIII

In what Places Wears shall be put down

All Wears from henceforth shall be utterly put down by *Thames* and *Medway*, and through all *England*, but only by the Sea-coasts.

CAP. XXIV

In what Case a Praecipe in Capite *is not grantable*

The Writ that is called *Praecipe in capite* shall be from henceforth granted to no person of any freehold, whereby any freeman may lose his Court.

CAP. XXV

There shall be but one Measure throughout the Realm

One measure of Wine shall be through our Realm, and one measure of Ale, and one measure of Corn, that is to say, the Quarter of *London*; and one breadth of dyed Cloth, Russets, and Haberjects, that is to say, two Yards within the lists. (2) And it shall be of Weights as it is of Measures.

CAP. XXVI

Inquisition of Life and Member

Nothing from henceforth shall be given for a Writ of Inquisition, nor taken of him that prayeth Inquisition of Life, or of Member, but it shall be granted freely, and not denied.

CAP. XXVII

Tenure of the King in Socage, and of another
by Knights Service. Petit Serjeanty

If any do hold of us by Fee-ferm, or by Socage, or Burgage, and he holdeth Lands of another by Knights Service, we will not have the Custody of his Heir, nor of his Land, which is holden of the Fee of another, by reason of that Fee-ferm, Socage, or Burgage. (2) Neither will we have the custody of such Fee-ferm, or Socage, or Burgage, except Knights Service be due unto us out of the same Fee-ferm. (3) We will not have the custody of the Heir, or of any Land, by occasion of any Petit Serjeanty, that any man holdeth of us by Service to pay a Knife, an Arrow, or the like.

CAP. XXVIII

Wager of Law shall not be without Witness

No Bailiff from henceforth shall put any man to his open Law, nor to an Oath, upon his own bare saying, without faithful Witnesses brought in for the same.

CAP. XXIX

None shall be condemned without Trial.
Justice shall not be sold or deferred

No Freeman shall be taken, or imprisoned, or be disseised of his Freehold, or Liberties, or free Customs, or be outlawed, or exiled, or any otherwise destroyed; *nor will we pass upon him, nor condemn him,* but by lawful Judgment of his Peers, or by the Law of the Land. (2) We will sell to no man, we will not deny or defer to any man either Justice or Right.

CAP. XXX

Merchant Strangers coming into this Realm
shall be well used

All Merchants (if they were not openly prohibited before) shall have their safe and sure Conduct to depart out of *England*, to come into *England*, to tarry in, and go through *England*, as well by Land as by Water, to buy and sell without any manner of evil Tolts, by the old and rightful Customs, except in Time of War. (2) And if they be of a land making War against us, and such be found in our Realm at the beginning of the Wars, they shall be attached without harm of body or goods, until it be known unto us, or our Chief Justice, how our Merchants be intreated there in the land making War against us; (3) and if our Merchants be well intreated there, theirs shall be likewise with us.

CAP. XXXI

Tenure of a Barony coming into the King's Hands by Eschete

If any man hold of any Eschete, as of the honour of *Wallingford, Nottingham, Boloin,* or of any other Eschetes which be in our hands, and are Baronies, and die, his Heir shall give none other Relief, nor do none other Service to us, than he should to the Baron, if it were in the Baron's hand. (2) And we in the same wise shall hold it as the Baron held it; neither shall we have, by occasion of any such Barony or Eschete, any Eschete or keeping of any of our men, unless he that held the Barony or Eschete hold of us in chief.

CAP. XXXII

Lands shall not be alienated to the Prejudice of the Lord's Service

No Freeman from henceforth shall give or sell any more of his Land, but so that of the residue of the Lands the Lord of the Fee may have the Service due to him, which belongeth to the Fee.

CAP. XXXIII

Patrons of Abbies shall have the Custody of them in the time of Vacation

All Patrons of Abbies, which have the King's Charters of *England* of Advowson, or have old Tenure or Possession in the same, shall have the Custody of them when they fall void, as it hath been accustomed, and as it is afore declared.

CAP. XXXIV

*In what Case only a Woman shall have
an Appeal of Death*

No Man shall be taken or imprisoned upon the Appeal of a Woman for the Death of any other, than of her husband.

CAP. XXXV

*At what Time shall be kept a County Court,
Sheriff's Turn, and a Leet*

No County Court from henceforth shall be holden, but from Month to Month; and where greater time hath been used, there shall be greater: Nor any Sheriff, or his Bailiff, shall keep his Turn in the Hundred but twice in the Year; and nowhere but in due place, and accustomed; that is to say, once after *Easter*, and again after the Feast of St. *Michael*. And the View of Frankpledge shall be likewise at the Feast of St. *Michael* without occasion; so that every man may have his Liberties which he had, or used to have, in the time of King HENRY our Grandfather, or which he hath purchased since: but the View of Frankpledge shall be so done, that our Peace may be kept; and that the Tything be wholly kept as it hath been accustomed; and that the Sheriff seek no Occasions, and that he be content with so much as the Sheriff was wont to have for his Viewmaking in the time of King HENRY our Grandfather.

CAP. XXXVI

No Land shall be given in Mortmain

It shall not be lawful from henceforth to any to give his Lands to any Religious House, and to take the same Land again to hold of the same House. Nor shall it be lawful to any House of Religion to take the Lands of any, and to lease the same to him of whom he received it. If any from henceforth give his Lands to any Religious House, and thereupon be convict, the Gift shall be utterly void, and the Land shall accrue to the Lord of the Fee.

CAP. XXXVII

A Subsidy in respect of this Charter, and the Charter of the Forest, granted to the King

Escuage from henceforth shall be taken like as it was wont to be in the time of King HENRY our Grandfather; reserving to all Archbishops, Bishops, Abbots, Priors, Templers, Hospitallers, Earls, Barons, and all persons, as well Spiritual as Temporal, all their free liberties and free Customs, which they have had in time passed. And all these Customs and Liberties aforesaid, which we have granted to be holden within this our Realm, as much as appertaineth to us *and our Heirs, we shall observe*; and all Men of this our Realm, as well Spiritual as Temporal (as much as in them is) shall observe the same against all persons in like wise. And for this our Gift and Grant of these Liberties, and of other contained in our Charter of Liberties of our Forest, the Archbishops, Bishops, Abbots, Priors, Earls, Barons, Knights, Freeholders, and other our Subjects, have given unto us the Fifteenth Part of all their Moveables. And we have granted unto them for us and our Heirs, that neither we, nor our Heirs shall procure or do anything whereby the Liberties in this Charter contained shall be infringed or broken; and if anything be procured by any person contrary to the premisses, it shall be had of no force nor effect. These being Witnesses; Lord B. Archbishop of *Canterbury*, E. Bishop of *London*, J. Bishop of *Bathe*, P. of *Winchester*, H. of *Lincoln*, R. of *Salisbury*, W. of *Rochester*, W. of *Worcester*, J. of *Ely*, H. of *Hereford*, R. of *Chichester*, W. of *Exeter*, Bishops;

the Abbot of St. *Edmunds*, the Abbot of St. *Albans*, the Abbot of *Bello*, the Abbot of St. *Augustines* in *Canterbury*, the Abbot of *Evesham*, the Abbot of *Westminster*, the Abbot of *Bourgh* St. *Peter*, the Abbot of *Reading*, the Abbot of *Abindon*, the Abbot of *Malmsbury*, the Abbot of *Winchcomb*, the Abbot of *Hyde*, the Abbot of *Certefey*, the Abbot of *Sherburn*, the Abbot of *Cerne*, the Abbot of *Abbotebir*, the Abbot of *Middleton*, the Abbot of *Seleby*, the Abbot of *Cirencester*; H. *de Burgh* Justice, H. Earl of *Chester* and *Lincoln*, W. Earl of *Salisbury*, W. Earl of *Warren*, G. *de Clare* Earl of *Gloucester* and *Hereford*, W. *de Ferrars* Earl of *Derby*, W. *de Mandeville* Earl of *Essex*, H. *de Bygod* Earl of *Norfolk*, W. Earl of *Albermarle*, H. Earl of *Hereford*, J. Constable of *Chester*, R. *de Ros*, R. *Fitzwalter*, R. *de Vyponte*, W. *de Bruer*, R. *de Muntefichet*, P. *Fitzherbert*, W. *de Aubenie*, F. *Grefly*, F. *de Breus*, J. *de Monemue*, J. *Fitzallen*, H. *de Mortimer*, W. *de Beauchamp*, W. *de St. John*, P. *de Mauly*, Brian *de Lisle*, *Thomas de Multon*, R. *de Argenteyn*, G. *de Nevil*, W. *de Mauduit*, J. *de Balun*, and others.

II. We, ratifying and approving these Gifts and Grants aforesaid, confirm and make strong all the same for us and our Heirs perpetually, and, by the Tenour of these Presents, do renew the same; willing and granting for us and our Heirs, that this Charter, and all and singular his Articles, for ever shall be stedfastly, firmly, and inviolably observed; *although some Articles in the same Charter contained, yet hitherto peradventure have not been kept, we will, and by Authority* Royal command, from henceforth firmly they be observed. In witness whereof we have caused these our Letters Patents to be made. T. EDWARD our Son at *Westminster, the Twenty-eighth Day* of March, *in the Twenty-eighth Year of our Reign.*

Bibliography

I. PRIMARY SOURCES

Unless otherwise stated, the place of publication is London

ANON., *Vox Plebis* (1646).
—— *Plain Truth, without Feare or Flattery* (1647).
—— *The Representative of Divers well-affected Persons in and about the City of London* (1649).
—— *Tryal and Condemnation of Fitzharris* (1681).
—— *A Defence of the Majority in the House of Commons on the Question relating to General Warrants* (1765).
—— *Historical Essay on the English Constitution* (1771).
ATWOOD, W., *Jus Anglorum ab Antiquo* (1681).
AUSTIN, J., *Lectures on Jurisprudence* (4th edn., 1879).
BACON, F., *Works*, ed. Spedding, Ellis, and Heath (1857–74), 7 vols.
—— *Letters and Life*, ed. Spedding (1861–72), 7 vols.
BENTHAM, J., *Works*, ed. J. Bowring (New York, 1962), 11 vols.
BLACKSTONE, W., *Commentaries on the Laws of England*, ed. T. M. Cooley (Chicago, 3rd edn., 1884), 4 vols.
—— *The Great Charter and the Charter of the Forest*, Law Tracts (Oxford, 1762), Vol. II.
BOLINGBROKE, H. St. J., *Works* (1809), 8 vols.
—— *A Collection of Political Tracts* (1769).
BRADY, R., *A Full and Clear Answer to a Book written by William Petit* (1681).
—— *A Complete History of England* (1685).
BURGH, J., *Political Disquisitions* (1774–5), 3 vols.
BURKE, E., *Works* (1808), 12 vols.
BURNET, G., *History of His Own Time* (1724), 2 vols.
CANNING, G., *Speeches, with a memoir by R. Therry* (1828), 6 vols.
CARLYLE, T., *The Letters and Speeches of Oliver Cromwell*, ed. S. C. Lomas (1904), 3 vols.
CARTWRIGHT, J., *American Independence* (1774).
—— *Take your Choice* (1776).
—— *An Appeal on the Subject of the English Constitution* (Boston, 1797).
—— *Letter to the Electors of Nottingham* (1803).
CLARENDON, EARL OF, EDWARD HYDE, *History of the Rebellion and Civil Wars in England* (1707), 3 vols.
Clarke Papers, ed. C. H. Firth (Camden Society, 1891–1901), 4 vols.
COBBETT, W., *A History of the last hundred days of English Freedom* (1820).
—— *Parliamentary History from 1066 to 1803* (1806–20), 12 vols.
COKE, E., *Institutes of the Laws of England* (1797), 4 parts.

COKE, E., *Reports* (1738), 13 parts.

COKE, R., *A Detection of the Court and State of England during the four last reigns and Interregnum* (1694), 2 vols.

COLLIER, J., *Vindiciae Juris Regii* (1689).

DE LOLME, J. L., *The Constitution of England* (1775).

EDWARDS, T., *Gangraena* (1646), 3 parts.

FILMER, R., *Patriarcha and other Political Works*, ed. P. Laslett (Oxford, 1949).

GREY, A., *Debates of the House of Commons, 1667–1694* (1769), 10 vols.

HALE, M., *History of the Common Law of England* (1713).

HALIFAX, MARQUIS OF, GEORGE SAVILE, *Complete Works*, ed. W. Raleigh (Oxford, 1912).

HALLER, W., *Tracts on Liberty in the Puritan Revolution, 1638–1647* (New York, 1934), contains in Vol. III, R. Overton's *Commons Complaint* and W. Walwyn's *England's Lamentable Slavery*.

—— and DAVIES, G., *The Leveller Tracts, 1647–1653* (New York, 1944), contains *The Earnest Petition of many freeborn people* and J. Lilburne's *The Just Defence*.

HANSARD, *Parliamentary Debates*, 1803–1820, 41 vols.

—— *Parliamentary Debates*, new series, 1820–1830, 25 vols.

—— *Parliamentary Debates*, third series, 1830–1891, 156 vols.

—— *Parliamentary Debates*, fourth series, 1892–1908, 198 vols.

—— *Parliamentary Debates*, fifth series, 1909 onwards (divided into Lords and Commons).

HARE, J., *England's proper and onely way to an establishment in honour, freedom, peace and happiness* (1648).

Harleian Miscellany (1808–13), contains in Vol. II, M. Nedham's *Short History of the English Rebellion*; in Vol. III, J. Ware's *The Corruption and Deficiency of the Laws of England*; in Vol. IV, W. Cole's *A Rod for the Lawyers*; in Vol. V, W. Raleigh's *The Prerogative of Parliament*; in Vol. VIII, S. Chidley's *A Cry against a Crying Sin*.

HERLE, C., *Ahab's Fall by his Prophets Flatteries* (1644).

HOBBES, T., *English Works*, ed. W. Molesworth (1839–45), 11 vols.

JOHNSON, Dr. S., *Works*, ed. A. Murphy (1824), 12 vols.

JOHNSON, S., *Second Part of the Confutation of the Ballancing Letter* (1700).

JOHNSTON, N., *The Excellency of Monarchical Government* (1686).

Journal of the House of Commons.

Journal of the House of Lords.

Journal of Sir Simonds D'Ewes, 1640–1641, ed. W. Notestein (New Haven, Conn., 1923).

LAUD, W., *Works*, ed. W. Scott and J. Bliss (Oxford, 1847–60), 7 vols.

Letters and Papers, Foreign and Domestic, of the Reign of Henry VIII, ed. J. S. Brewer, J. Gairdner, and R. H. Brodie (1862–1932), 21 vols.

LILBURNE, J., *A Copy of a Letter to a Friend* (1645).

—— *The Freemans Freedom Vindicated* (1646).

—— *A Just Mans Justification* (1647).

—— *Jonah's Cry out of the Whales Belly* (1647).

LILBURNE, J., *Regall Tyrannie Discovered* (1647).
—— *The Peoples Prerogative and Priviledges asserted and vindicated* (1648).
—— *The Prisoners Plea for a Habeas Corpus* (1648).
—— *A Discourse betwixt John Lilburne and Hugh Peters* (1649).
—— *A Remonstrance of Lieut. Col. John Lilburne: concerning the Laws, Liberties, and Inheritances of the freeborn people of England* (1652).
—— *An Hue and Cry after the Fundamental Lawes and Liberties of England* (1653).
LOCKE, J., *Two Treatises of Government*, ed. P. Laslett (Cambridge, 2nd edn., 1967).
LOVETT, W., *Life and Struggles* (1876).
LUDLOW, E., *Memoirs*, ed. C. H. Firth (Oxford, 1894), 2 vols.
MACAULAY, T. B., *Selected Speeches*, ed. G. M. Young (1935).
MACKINTOSH, J., *Vindiciae Gallicae* (1791).
—— *History of England* (1830), 3 vols.
MILLAR, J., *An Historical View of the English Government* (1787).
Mirror of Justices, ed. W. J. Whittacker (Selden Society, 1895).
PAINE, T., *Selected Works of Tom Paine*, ed. H. Fast (New York, 1945).
PARKER, H., *The True Grounds of Ecclesiastical Regiment* (1641).
—— *Animadversions Animadverted* (1642).
—— *Observations upon some of his Majesties late Answers and Expresses* (1642).
—— *Contra Replicant* (1643).
PEPYS, S., *Diary* (1906 reprint of 1848 edn.).
PHILIPPS, F., *The Established Government of England, vindicated from All popular and republican Principles and Mistakes: with respect to the Laws of God, Man, Nature and Nations* (1687).
Political Works of James I, ed. C. H. McIlwain (Cambridge, Mass., 1918).
PRICE, R., *Observations on the Nature of Civil Liberty* (2nd edn., 1776).
PRYNNE, W., *Lyar Confounded* (1645).
Public General Acts.
ROBINSON, H., *Certaine proposals in order to a new modelling of the lawes* (1653).
ROPER, W., *Life of Sir Thomas More* (New York, 1962).
RUSHWORTH, J., *Historical Collections* (1721), 8 vols.
SABINE, G. H., *Works of Gerrard Winstanley* (New York, 1941).
Severall Proceedings in Parliament, 30 November–7 December, 1649, contains *The Humble Petition of the Lord Mayor, Aldermen and Commons of the City of London.*
SHARP, G., *A Declaration of the People's Natural Right to a Share in the Legislature* (1774).
Somers Tracts (2nd edn., 1809–15), contains in Vol. IV, *A Brief Relation of the death and sufferings of the most revered and renowned prelate, the Lord Archbishop of Canterbury*; in Vol. VI, *Several draughts of acts* and *An Exact Relation of the Proceedings and Transactions of the late Parliament*; in Vol. VIII, *England's concern in the Case of His Royal Highness, James, Duke of York* and *A Seasonable Address to both Houses of Parliament concerning the Succession*; in Vol. X, *Reflexions upon our late and present proceedings in England* and *Honesty is the best Policy.*

State Tracts, being a collection of several treatises relating to Government, 1660–1689 (1689–92), contains in Vol. I, *A relation of two free conferences between Father le Chese and four considerable Jesuits* and W. Atwood's *The Character of a Popish Successor*; in Vol. II, *Reflexions on Monsieur Fagel's Letter* and *Animadversions upon a pretended answer to Mijn Heer Fagel's Letter.*

State Trials, ed. T. B. and T. J. Howell (1816–28), 34 vols.

Statutes at Large, ed. O. Ruffhead, revised C. Runnington (1786–1800), 14 vols.

SWIFT, J., *Works* (Dublin, 1741–51), 9 vols.

THELWALL, J., *The Natural and Constitutional Rights of Britons* (1795).

The Statutes, revised edition (1870–1885), 18 vols.

The Statutes, 2nd revised edition (1888–1929), 24 vols.

The Statutes, 3rd revised edition (1950), 32 vols.

WALPOLE, H., *Journal of the Reign of George III,* ed. J. Doran (1859), 2 vols.

—— *Letters of H. Walpole,* ed. P. Toynbee (Oxford, 1903–25), 19 vols.

WOLFE, D. M., *Leveller Manifestoes of the Puritan Revolution* (New York, 1944), contains R. Overton's *A Remonstrance of many thousand citizens* and *An Appeale from the Commons to the Free People of England.*

WYVILL, C., *Political Papers* (York, 1794–1802), 6 vols.

NEWSPAPERS AND JOURNALS

The Black Dwarf, ed. T. J. Wooler (1817–24).

The Daily Gazetteer (1735–48).

The London Journal (1720–34).

The Moderate (1648–9).

The North Briton, compiled by W. Bingley (2nd edn., 1771).

The Patriot (1792–3).

The Political Register, ed. W. Cobbett (1802–35).

The Reformer's Register (1817).

II. SECONDARY AUTHORITIES

BELOFF, M. (ed.), *The Debate on the American Revolution* (1949).

BRIGGS, A. (ed.), *Chartist Studies* (1959).

BROWN, W. J., *The Austinian Theory of Law* (1906).

BUTTERFIELD, H., *The Englishman and his History* (Cambridge, 1944).

—— *George III, Lord North and the People, 1779–1780* (1948).

—— *Magna Carta in the historiography of the sixteenth and seventeenth centuries* (Reading, Stenton Lecture, 1969).

CAMPBELL, J., *Lives of the Chief Justices of England* (3rd edn., 1874), 4 vols.

CHRISTIE, I. R., *Wilkes, Wyvill and Reform* (1962).

COBBAN, A., *Edmund Burke and the Revolt against the Eighteenth Century* (1929).

COTTERELL, M., 'Interregnum Law Reform: the Hale Commission of 1652', 83 *E.H.R.* (1968), 689 ff.

DICEY, A. V., *Introduction to the Study of the Law of the Constitution* (10th edn., 1959).

DUNNING, W. A., 'Truth in History', 19 *Am. H.R.* (1924), 217 ff.

FORBES, D., 'Historismus in England', 4 *Cambridge Journal* (1951), 387 ff.

FOSS, E., *Judges of England* (1848–64), 9 vols.

FOXCROFT, H. C. (ed.), *The Life and Letters of Sir George Savile* (1898), 2 vols.

GEORGE, M. D., *English Political Caricature*, Vol. I: *To 1792*, Vol. II: *1793–1832* (Oxford, 1959).

GOUGH, J. W., *Fundamental Law in English Constitutional History* (Oxford, 1955).

GUTTRIDGE, G. H., *English Whiggism and the American Revolution* (Berkeley, Cal., 1942).

HAMSON, C. J., *Executive Discretion and Judicial Control* (1954).

HEWART, G., *The New Despotism* (1929).

HOLDSWORTH, W. S., *History of the English Law* (1922–66), 16 vols.

HOLMES, G., *British Politics in the Age of Anne* (1967).

HOLT, J. C., *Magna Carta* (Cambridge, 1965).

—— 'Magna Carta: Law and Constitution', *Listener*, 8 July 1965.

—— 'Magna Carta and the Origin of Statute Law', *Essays in Honour of Gaines Post*, ed. D. E. Queller (Princeton, N.J., forthcoming).

HOWARD, A. E. DICK, *The Road from Runnymede: Magna Carta and American Constitutionalism* (Charlottesville, Va., 1968).

JORDAN, W. K., *Men of Substance: a study of the thought of two English Revolutionaries, Henry Parker and Henry Robinson* (Chicago, 1942).

JUDSON, M. A., 'Henry Parker and the Theory of Parliamentary Sovereignty', *Essays in History and Political Theory in Honour of C. H. McIlwain* (Cambridge, Mass., 1936).

KIRK, R., 'Burke and the Philosophy of Prescription', 14 *Journal of the History of Ideas* (1953), 365 ff.

KRAMNICK, I., 'Augustan Politics and English Historiography', 6 *History and Theory* (1967), 33 ff.

—— *Bolingbroke and his Circle* (Cambridge, Mass., 1968).

LIDDEN, H. P., *Life of E. B. Pusey* (1893–7), 4 vols.

McILWAIN, C. H., *The High Court of Parliament* (New Haven, Conn., 1910).

MACKAY, R. A., 'Coke—Parliamentary Sovereignty or the Supremacy of the Law?', 22 *Michigan Law Review* (1923–4), 215 ff.

McKECHNIE, W. S., *Magna Carta* (Glasgow, 2nd edn., 1924).

MACPHERSON, C. B., *The Political Theory of Possessive Individualism* (Oxford, 1962).

MALDEN, H. E. (ed.), *Magna Carta Commemorative Essays* (1917).

MERRIAM, C. E., *History of the Theory of Sovereignty since Rousseau* (New York, 1900).

MERRIMAN, R. B. (ed.), *Life and Letters of Thomas Cromwell* (Oxford, 1902), 2 vols.

MITCHELL, J. D. B., 'The Constitutional Implications of Judicial Control', 25 *Cambridge Law Journal* (1967), 46 ff.

MULLETT, C. F., *Fundamental Law and the American Revolution, 1760–1776* (New York, 1933).

NEWMAN, A. N., *The Stanhopes of Chevening* (1969).

NOURSE, G. B., 'Law Reform under the Commonwealth and Protectorate', 75 *L.Q.R.* (1959), 512 ff.

PLUCKNETT, T. F. T., 'Bonham's Case and Judicial Review', 40 *Harvard Law Review* (1926), 30 ff.

POCOCK, J. G. A., 'Robert Brady', 10 *Cambridge Historical Journal* (1951), 186 ff.

—— *The Ancient Constitution and the Feudal Law* (Cambridge, 1957).

—— 'Burke and the Ancient Constitution', 3 *Historical Journal* (1960), 125 ff.

SCARMAN, L., 'Law Reform—The Experience of the Law Commission', 10 *Journal of the Society of Public Teachers of Law* (1968), 91 ff.

STREET, H., *Justice in the Welfare State* (1968).

SUTHERLAND, D. W., *Quo Warranto Proceedings in the Reign of Edward I, 1278–1294* (Oxford, 1963).

THOMPSON, F., *The First Century of Magna Carta: Why it Persisted as a Document* (Minneapolis, 1925).

—— *Magna Carta: Its Role in the Making of the English Constitution, 1300–1629* (Minneapolis, 1948).

THORNE, S. E., 'The Constitution and the Courts', 54 *L.Q.R.* (1938), 543 ff.

—— *Sir Edward Coke, 1552–1952* (Selden Society Lecture, 1952).

VEAL, D., *The Popular Movement for Law Reform, 1640–1660* (Oxford, 1970).

WADE, H. W. R., 'The Myth of Unfettered Discretion', 84 *L.Q.R.* (1968), 166 ff.

WILLIAMS, D. G. T., *Not in the Public Interest* (1965).

Index

Coke, E. (*cont.*):
  influence of, 5, 9, 19, 21, 23, 50, 52,
    58, 68, 79 n., 80, 85
Cole, W., 91
Collier, J., 33
Colville of Culross, 4th Viscount, 99
Convention Parliament (1660), 26, 40
Convention Parliament (1689), 40, 65 n.
Cony, G., 24
Coronation Oath, 32, 36
County Association Movement, 65
Craftsman, The, 53
Criminal Law Act (1967), 99
Cromwell, O., 16, 24, 25 n., 90 n., 92
Cromwell, T., 101 n.
Crown privilege, 105
Crown Proceedings Act (1947), 97
Custom, 2, 6, 13, 87

Daily Gazetteer, The, 53–4
Danby, T. Osborne, 1st Earl of, 28, 30
Darling, Mr. Justice, 103 n., 104
Declaration of Rights, 41, 49, 82
Declarations of Indulgence, 38–9
Declaratory Bill (America), 56, 64 n.
Defence of the Realm regulations, 103
Defoe, D., 49–50
Delegated legislation, 103–4
De Lolme, J. L., 5–6
Denning, Lord, 1, 102 n.
Dicey, A. V., 44, 46 n.
Diggers, The, 22, 25
Discretionary powers, 104–5
Divine right, 36–7
Dunning's motion, 66

Edward I, King of England, 79
Edwards, T., 22
Egerton, T., 90
Elizabeth I, Queen of England, 89
Elton, G. R., 101 n.
Emergency Powers (Defence) Act
  (1939), 104 n.
Equitable justice, 6, 9, 106
Equity, 3, 18–22 *passim*, 76, 91
Exclusion, 37–8

Fielden, J., 75
Filmer, R., 3 n., 24, 32
Fitzharris, E., 28, 29 n.
Forbes, D., 78 n.
French Revolution, 5, 76, 77, 80

General Warrants, 59, 60 n.
George III, King of England, 54, 64
Gough, J. W., 46, 47 n.
Guttridge, G. H., 54, 55

Habeas Corpus Act (1679), 31, 45, 70–1
  suspensions of, 44 n., 70, 103
Habeas corpus writ, 24, 31–2, 60
Hale, M., 30 n., 32, 92
Halifax, G. Savile, 1st Marquis of, 39
Hampden Club, 70
Hare, J., 90 n.
Hennessy, P., 96
Henry I, King of England, 2, 34, 79
Henry III, King of England, 2, 34, 79
Herbert Commission, 102
Herle, C., 11
Hewart, G., 103 n.
Historical Essay on the English Constitution, 64
Historical School, 77–82 *passim*
Hobbes, T., 3 n., 12 n., 25, 77, 86–7
Holdsworth, W., 30 n., 46
Holt, J. C., 2 n., 28 n., 84 n.
Hutcheson, A., 45

Impeachments:
  Clarendon, 27–8
  Mordaunt, 27 n.
  Danby, 28
  Fitzharris, 28
  Scroggs, 31
Independents, The, 13, 14
Interregnum, 25, 90, 92, 93
Ireton, H., 14, 21

James I, King of England, 9, 10, 90
James II, King of England, 31, 37–40
  passim
John, King of England, 1, 2, 34, 62,
  78–9
Johnson, Dr. S., 55
Johnson, S., 2
Johnston, N., 32 n., 34 n.
Joint Committee of Lords and Commons on Consolidation Bills, 100–1
Jones, G., 68–9
Jones, W., 29
Jordan, W. K., 12 n.
Judicial review, 104–6
Judiciary, 17, 21, 29, 83
Judson, M. A., 13 n.
Jura Populi Anglicani, 50

PRINTED IN GREAT BRITAIN
AT THE UNIVERSITY PRESS, OXFORD
BY VIVIAN RIDLER
PRINTER TO THE UNIVERSITY

Magna Carta

THE HERITAGE OF LIBERTY